VEGAN MEAL PREP

A 5-WEEK PLAN WITH 125 READY-TO-GO RECIPES

ROBIN ASBELL

Robert
ROSE

DESIGN AND PRODUCTION: Kevin Cockburn/PageWave Graphics Inc.
EDITOR: Sue Sumeraj
RECIPE EDITOR: Jennifer MacKenzie
PROOFREADER: Kelly Jones
INDEXER: Gillian Watts

COVER IMAGE: Westend61/Getty Images

PHOTOGRAPHS:
page 3: © iStockphoto.com/Creative-Family; page 13: © istockphoto.com/showcake; page 16: © iStockphoto.com/Foxys_forest_manufacture;
page 19: © iStockphoto.com/nebari; page 20: © iStockphoto.com/los_angela; page 23: © iStockphoto.com/PoppyB;
page 31: © iStockphoto.com/fcafotodigital; page 38: © iStockphoto.com/Roxiller; page 45: © iStockphoto.com/4kodiak;
page 69: © iStockphoto.com/HeikeRau; page 70: © iStockphoto.com/ArxOnt; page 98: © iStockphoto.com/saschanti;
page 126 © iStockphoto.com/nerudol ; page 154: © iStockphoto.com/vicuschka; page 168: © iStockphoto.com/mpessaris

Published by Robert Rose Inc.
120 Eglinton Avenue East, Suite 800, Toronto, Ontario, Canada M4P 1E2
Tel: (416) 322-6552 Fax: (416) 322-6936
www.robertrose.ca

Printed and bound in Canada

1 2 3 4 5 6 7 8 9 TCP 27 26 25 24 23 22 21 20 19

CONTENTS

SETTING YOURSELF UP FOR SUCCESS: FIVE WEEKS OF VEGAN MEALS 4

MEAL PREP 101: PLANNING, SHOPPING AND PREPPING 14

LET'S GET COOKING! 125 VEGAN RECIPES 37

5 WEEKS OF VEGAN MEALS

Want to go vegan and eat unprocessed whole foods? You might think changing your eating habits will involve spending hours in the kitchen or a bundle on exotic ingredients, but with the help of this book, you can meet your goals and eat a plant-based diet without slaving away every night or breaking the bank at the health food store.

When it comes to eating, you definitely need a plan. Hunger comes whether you are ready or not. If you don't have a good choice already in place, your hunger will drive you to the easiest option. In our fast-paced world, it's too easy to fall into eating fast food, packaged food and junk food. And if you are trying to avoid animal products, you are doubly challenged, as even the best restaurants have limited options for you. Whether you are an experienced vegan devotee or just want to try going vegan for five weeks, the *Vegan Meal Prep* plan will make it much easier to eat well. With this plan, you cook once a week so that you can open the fridge after a long day of work and have a head start.

Having a plan sets you up for success. Prepping means your mealtime decisions are made in advance, and meals that fit your goals will now be the easiest option facing you, because the components will be ready to go in your refrigerator. In the time it would take to call in your pizza delivery order and wait for it to arrive, you can make a fresh, hot, plant-based meal — tips optional!

WHAT IS MEAL PREP?

WHEN YOU ORDER FOOD at a restaurant, you are reaping the benefits of meal prep. Restaurants prep your food in advance so they can get it out to you in a reasonable amount of time. Starting early in the morning and working all day long, prep cooks at the back of the house are chopping vegetables, making sauces, dressings and marinades, and partially cooking foods to be finished at the last minute by the line cooks. Without this prep, meals would take hours to make it to the table.

In your home kitchen, you can take on the role of the prep cook one day of the week, then step into the shoes of the line cook for the next five days. The upside is that you will work very short shifts and won't have a chef barking orders. All the food will be for you, so you can tweak the seasonings to suit yourself and your family.

To quote Dorothy Parker, "Eternity is two people and a ham." A ham won't help with vegan meal planning, but you can make sure you have plenty of plant-based protein prepped. When I was a broke college student, a crockpot full of bean and vegetable soup was often dinner for the whole week, repetitive as it was. For me, eternity was four roommates and a pot of soup.

That pot of soup taught me a lesson. Out of sheer boredom, I started giving each night's portion a different flavor profile. I added curry powder and coconut, or chili powder and tomatoes, and suddenly my soup was different enough to keep my interest. With a few minutes in the kitchen, I could accessorize with a quick bread or make my stroke of genius "toaster croutons" by chopping up toast. I was meal prepping to survive and didn't really know it.

Don't worry — the meal plan in this book is not about eating one pot of soup all week. It's about shaving time from your weeknight meal preparations by preparing beans, grains and vegetables in advance so they are ready to be assembled into tasty meals. Add a sauce, a salad dressing, some breakfast options and maybe a treat, and you have a time-saving gold mine in your refrigerator.

Pick a day of the week that works for you, follow the steps laid out for each week and in the time it takes to binge-watch a few episodes of *Game of Thrones*, you'll be all set up to eat right. With a little planning, you'll be getting breakfast, lunch and dinner on the table in minutes. I've even given you some great vegan dessert and snack recipes, to keep your sweet tooth happy while you're eating wholesome vegan treats!

ROASTING VEGGIES

Roasting vegetables is a strategy that works year-round, shrinking large quantities of veggies into easy-to-store, ready-to-eat prepped foods. In the summer you can switch to cutting up veggies and storing them to steam or eat raw.

WHY PREP?

MANY PEOPLE DECIDE to make a change in their eating habits, only to fall back into their old ways within days. You'll sometimes hear people say that eating vegan or giving up junk food or eating more healthfully in general is just too hard. These people just needed a meal prep plan. Eating differently from the people around you has its challenges, but by being your own prep cook, you make it easy on yourself.

Prepping won't just help you keep junk food at bay, it will also save you money. Making your own meals is always less expensive than going out to eat or picking up takeout. And shopping the bulk bins for your food prep is markedly less spendy than buying prepared foods in the deli or freezer aisles. Homemade dips, sauces and dressings are a bargain compared to packaged versions. You'll also be cutting way back on the amount of packaging you are paying for then tossing in the trash, which will help reduce your carbon footprint. Your meals will all be fresh and made to your taste, too.

AVOIDING GLUTEN If you're avoiding gluten or wheat, you can easily customize most of the recipes in this book by cooking gluten-free whole grains and buying gluten-free breads, tortillas and pasta.

WHY VEGAN?

YOU HAVE THIS BOOK in your hands because you are at least interested in eating a plant-based diet. There's a growing movement toward eating more plants and less animal food, for good reasons. Whether you are in this for your health, the environment or the animals, your vegan meal plan will have an impact.

EATING MORE PLANTS FOR HEALTH

The top cause of death worldwide is heart disease, followed closely by cancer. Eating more plants is a powerful way to reduce your risk factors for both of those diseases. Whether you are adopting a vegan diet and lifestyle or simply adding vegan meals to your omnivorous habits, you will reap great health benefits.

The vegan meal plans in this book are based on three of the more health-protective food groups we have: beans, whole grains, and vegetables and fruits. These delicious, beautiful foods are the basis of ancient foodways and have been enjoyed as daily staples for thousands of years by the longest-lived people.

Beans are high in protein, fiber, antioxidants, protein, B vitamins, iron, magnesium, potassium, copper and zinc. The soluble fiber in beans actually removes excess cholesterol from the body and decreases triglyceride levels, reducing the risk of heart disease. Simply replacing the meat and cheese in your diet with beans and other legumes, without making any other healthy changes, has been shown to result in a longer life and a healthier weight. That's probably because, when you replace protein from meat or cheese with beans, you are cutting out a food with no fiber, and often plenty of saturated fat, and replacing it with a fiber-rich, fat-free food.

Whole grains, like beans, have a long track record as highly health-promoting foods. While each grain has a different nutritional profile, all whole grains are higher in protein, fiber and minerals than their refined counterparts. Eating whole grains daily reduces your risk of stroke, heart disease, certain cancers, type 2 diabetes and inflammation. People who eat whole grains also maintain a healthy weight more easily, thanks to all that filling fiber. If you are accustomed to eating white-flour products, use this plan to switch over to whole wheat. You'll be buying some buns, breads and pasta, all of which are best when made with whole-grain, natural flours.

Of course, vegetables and fruits are essential to a healthy body, and most people don't eat enough of them. Following a vegan diet should mean that you are eating lots of vegetables. Vitamins, minerals, antioxidants, fiber — all kinds of health-promoting nutrients are concentrated in vegetables and fruits.

On top of that healthy foundation, you'll be eating nuts, seeds and reasonable amounts of healthy fats and sweeteners. Making your own meals means you can choose only the best ingredients.

WHOLE FOODS VEGAN

The food philosophy that guides this book is whole foods vegan, which means you won't be buying lots of processed foods. For some ethical vegans, all that matters is that a food is vegan, but a diet made up of processed vegan foods and deep-fried snacks is not sustainable. If you're going plant-based and eating lots of refined foods, packaged foods and treats, you might not reap the health benefits of the vegan lifestyle despite the change. A meal prep plan makes a whole-foods vegan diet easy and attainable.

THE ENVIRONMENT

Every time you choose to eat plants over animal foods, you are reducing your impact on the environment. To support our current way of eating, vast acreages of land are used to grow plants that are fed to animals. When those animals are slaughtered, their meat is refrigerated and shipped to stores and restaurants. We must be conscious of the true costs of animal foods, from start to finish. To produce a pound of beef, depending on who you ask, 1,300 to 1,700 gallons of water are used to water the plants the cow ate, give it drinking water and process the meat. If you add up all the energy costs that go into growing and transporting the food for the animal, caring for the animal and, of course, the processing, that adds both gallons of gas and the environmentally destructive emissions that come from burning it. Animal agriculture advocates like to argue the numbers, but it is obvious that protein from plant foods requires far less water and energy.

Raising animals also produces a huge amount of waste — manure and other byproducts that make their way into lakes and streams, kill the organisms living there and sicken the people who drink the water. We know that the methane produced by cows is harming the environment as well.

THE ANIMALS

We can live healthy, happy lives without eating animals or, for that matter, their milk and eggs. Contrary to popular belief, we don't need any animal foods to meet our nutritional requirements. For many vegans, it just feels better to stop participating in the brutal business of exploiting and slaughtering animals. Factory farms treat the animals like cogs in a machine, with no regard for their suffering, and the animals live very unnatural lives. Like our favorite household pets, pigs, chickens and cows deserve to be protected from cruel treatment. Many people who go vegan do so to live their values of compassion and kindness more fully.

VEGAN NUTRITION BASICS

IF YOU ARE NEW to veganism, there are a few key things to know. You might think that protein is going to be the hard part, but getting enough protein is actually relatively easy. There are a few other nutrients, however, that you need to be sure to get enough of. These include omega-3 fatty acids, vitamin B_{12}, vitamin D, calcium, iodine, iron and zinc.

FORTIFIED NONDAIRY MILKS

Because of the growing number of vegans, many nondairy milks are fortified with vitamins and other nutrients. We can thank the manufacturers of these milks for making it much easier for vegans to meet their nutrient needs. Not all nondairy milks are fortified, though, so read the label before you buy one.

PROTEIN

We live in a protein-obsessed age. Everyone is eating protein at the levels of Olympic athletes in the belief that it will make them leaner or stronger. The protein message is repeated so often, you might think you need protein powders and bars to survive a vegan lifestyle.

That couldn't be further from the truth. The current recommended daily allowance (RDA) for protein in the United States and Canada is 0.8 grams per kilogram of body weight per day. To convert your weight from pounds to kilograms, divide it by 2.2, then multiply that by 0.8 to get the amount of protein you should be consuming each day. For example, a 140-pound (63 kg) person needs 50 grams of protein per day.

If you look at the examples in the list below, you'll see that there are a few grams of protein in most whole foods, even broccoli, and they all add up. Don't worry about whether they are "complete" proteins — your body does a fine job of putting all the amino acids in the right place.

PROTEIN PER SERVING IN COMMON FOODS

Black beans (1 cup/250 mL cooked) .... 15.2 g
Chickpeas (1 cup/250 mL cooked) .... 14.5 g
Farro (1 cup/250 mL cooked) .... 12.0 g
Quinoa (1 cup/250 mL cooked) .... 8.1 g
Tofu (3½ oz/100 g) .... 8.1 g
Whole wheat bread (2 slices) .... 8.0 g
Soy milk (1 cup/250 mL) .... 6.3–8.0 g
Almonds (1 oz/30 g) .... 6.0 g
Large-flake (old-fashioned) rolled oats (1 cup/250 mL cooked) .... 5.9 g
Cashews (1 oz/30 g raw) .... 5.2 g
Tahini (2 tbsp/30 mL) .... 5.2 g
Brown rice, medium-grain (1 cup/250 mL cooked) .... 4.5 g
Potato (1 medium, baked) .... 4.3 g
Broccoli (1 cup/250 mL chopped, raw) .... 2.5 g
Banana (1 medium) .... 1.3 g

OMEGA-3 FATTY ACIDS

For your daily omega-3s, three walnut halves or a teaspoon (5 mL) of canola oil or ground flax seeds will meet your needs. There is no RDA for omega-3s in the United States or Canada, but the consensus is that 250 to 500 milligrams per day should do it.

 **OMEGA-6S** The oils used in this book — olive oil and canola oil — are low in omega-6 fatty acids and help give you the best balance of omega fats.

OMEGA 3S PER SERVING IN COMMON FOODS

Flaxseed oil (1 tsp/5 mL) .... 2460 mg
Flax seeds (1 tsp/5 mL ground) .... 2430 mg
Walnuts (¼ cup/60 mL chopped) .... 2300 mg
Walnut oil (1 tsp/5 mL) .... 480 mg
Tofu (5 oz/150 g) .... 250–480 mg
Canola oil (1 tsp/5 mL) .... 420 mg
Pecans (¼ cup/60 mL chopped) .... 250–290 mg

Avocado (1 medium)..221 mg

Kale (1 cup/250 mL cooked)...130 mg

Tempeh (3 oz/85 g)..120 mg

Broccoli (1 cup/250 mL chopped, cooked)...............................93 mg

VITAMIN B$_{12}$

Vitamin B$_{12}$ is the one vitamin that is present naturally only in animal foods. Guidelines published by the United States Department of Agriculture (USDA) and Health Canada say that adults need 2.4 micrograms (mcg) of vitamin B$_{12}$ per day. To get enough, you must consume fortified foods, like nutritional yeast, nondairy milks and cereals, or take supplements.

When purchasing nutritional yeast — affectionately called "nooch" by vegans — make sure it is Red Star Vegetarian Support Formula, not brewer's yeast or another yeast that doesn't have B$_{12}$. Keep your yeast in a cool, dark place.

Several brands of nondairy milk contain 50% of the RDA for vitamin B$_{12}$ per serving, so look for those.

If you are not eating nooch or other fortified foods daily, you might need to buy a supplement.

VITAMIN D

We get vitamin D from sunshine, but if you avoid sun exposure or live in a northern clime, you probably don't get enough sun to cover your daily needs. Dietary sources of vitamin D include fatty fish, eggs and mushrooms that have been exposed to sunlight or UV light. Since you're not eating fish and eggs, if you don't spend about half an hour a day in the sun, with your face and arms exposed, you probably need to consider selecting foods fortified with vitamin D and taking a supplement. The RDA for vitamin D in the United States and Canada is 600 international units (IU). Vitamin D$_2$ is always vegan, but vitamin D$_3$ can be derived from either sheep's wool or vegan-friendly lichen, so check the label.

CALCIUM

Replacing the calcium in dairy is easy enough if you buy calcium-fortified nondairy milks, eat tofu coagulated with calcium and eat plenty of spinach, kale, mustard greens, collards and watercress. The RDA in the United States and Canada for men and women over 18 is 1,000 milligrams, and it's higher for adolescents and seniors.

CALCIUM PER SERVING IN COMMON FOODS

Blackstrap molasses (2 tbsp/30 mL)..400 mg

Tofu prepared with calcium sulfate (3$\frac{1}{2}$ oz/100 g) ....350 mg

Orange juice, calcium-fortified (1 cup/250 mL)..............................349 mg

Soy milk, calcium-fortified, plain (1 cup/250 mL)...........................299 mg

Collard greens (1 cup/250 mL cooked).......................................268 mg

Spinach (1 cup/250 mL cooked)...245 mg

Kale (1 cup/250 mL cooked) ....177 mg

Tahini (2 tbsp/30 mL) ....130 mg

Almonds (¼ cup/60 mL whole)..96 mg

IODINE

Iodine is found in fish, dairy and eggs, so when you give those up, you need to be sure to find vegan sources. Iodized salt is one way to make sure you are getting enough iodine. Eating seaweeds like nori and dulse several times per week can do it too. Iodine deficiency can cause thyroid problems, so if you aren't using iodized salt, try a supplement.

IRON

Iron deficiency is very common, even among omnivores. The RDA for iron in the United States and Canada for women over 18 is 18 milligrams, while men need 8 milligrams. The best way to get plenty of iron is to eat whole foods. Foods containing vitamin C help you absorb iron, so eat them at the same time. The legumes and whole grains you will be prepping are good sources of iron. Nuts and seeds are too. Eating vegetables and salads is a natural way to get vitamin C and iron at the same meal. Cook in cast-iron pans, and you'll be adding iron to all your meals.

IRON PER SERVING IN COMMON FOODS

Raisin bran flakes cereal (1 cup/250 mL)....................................10.8 mg

Blackstrap molasses (2 tbsp/30 mL)..7.2 mg

Lentils (1 cup/250 mL cooked)..6.6 mg

Spinach (1 cup/250 mL cooked)...6.4 mg

Kidney beans (1 cup/250 mL cooked)..5.2 mg

Chickpeas (1 cup/250 mL cooked)...4.7 mg

Lima beans (1 cup/250 mL cooked)..4.5 mg

Swiss chard (1 cup/250 mL cooked)...4.0 mg

Edamame (1 cup/250 mL cooked)...3.5 mg

Green pumpkin seeds (¼ cup/60 mL)...2.9 mg

Quinoa (1 cup/250 mL cooked)..2.8 mg

Tahini (2 tbsp/30 mL) ....2.7 mg

Cashews (1 oz/30 g)..1.9 mg

Whole wheat bread (2 slices) ....1.6 mg

Brown rice (1 cup/250 mL cooked)..1.0 mg

ZINC

Because you are eating whole foods, getting enough zinc should be no problem. Legumes, nuts, seeds, oats, whole-grain breads, tempeh and miso are all sources of zinc. Women over 18 need 8 milligrams of zinc per day, while men need 11 milligrams.

ZINC PER SERVING IN COMMON FOODS

Hemp seeds (3 tbsp/45 mL)	3.0 mg
Green pumpkin seeds (1/4 cup/60 mL)	2.5 mg
Lentils (1 cup/250 mL cooked)	2.5 mg
Large-flake (old-fashioned) rolled oats (1 cup/250 mL cooked)	2.3 mg
Wild rice (1 cup/250 mL)	2.2 mg
Cashews (1 oz/28 g)	1.6 mg
Tempeh (3 1/2 oz/100 g)	1.1 mg
Whole wheat bread (2 slices)	1.1 mg
Miso (2 tbsp/30 mL)	0.9 mg
Tofu (3 1/2 oz/100 g)	0.8 mg

INTRO TO VEGAN SHOPPING

IF YOU ARE NEW to vegan shopping, there are a few ins and outs to know — nothing too difficult, but at the beginning, you will be reading labels carefully. You may start shopping at more vegan-friendly stores or making the occasional trip to the Asian market for mock duck and tofu.

SWEETENERS

When shopping for vegan sweeteners, you might feel a little overwhelmed. The first thing you need to know is that conventional granulated sugar and brown sugar are not considered vegan because, to make sugar, cow bones are recycled into charcoal and used to filter the cane juice. Any sugar labeled "organic" has been processed without animal products, so look for organic sugars if you want to follow a true vegan diet. However, either conventional or organic granulated and brown sugars will work in the recipes in this book.

Coconut sugar, or palm sugar, is the concentrated juice of the coconut palm. It is made in much the same way as maple syrup, with delicious results. Soft palm sugar can be substituted for brown sugar in these recipes. Rapadura, also called panela, is one of the least refined sweeteners made from sugar cane, made by simply boiling and drying cane juice, with no nutrients removed. It's a bit chunky, so to use it in these recipes, buzz it in a mini chopper or food processor, or with an immersion blender, to powder it more finely, then use it as you would brown sugar.

Beyond sugar, there are many alternative and natural sweeteners to choose from. Maple syrup is a whole, unrefined product that retains nutrients from the maple tree. Because the tree is tapped, the environmental impact is low and the process is sustainable. Agave nectar is another natural sweetener that is often recommended by nutritionists because it is lower on the glycemic index than sugar. It can be swapped for maple syrup if you want to use it in these recipes.

AVOIDING ANIMAL PRODUCTS

Because you are eating mostly whole foods, you will be sidestepping many of the hidden animal foods found in processed food items. Reading labels will help you avoid buying ingredients that contain less obvious animal products. Here are some potential pitfalls to be aware of:

- **CURRY PASTE:** Avoid buying curry pastes that contain shrimp or fish, or those where the ingredient list includes a vague term like "condiment."
- **FISH SAUCE:** Some favorite Thai and Vietnamese foods are seasoned with fish sauce, so look out for that. Use tamari or another soy sauce instead of fish sauce.
- **BREADS:** Some breads contain milk, eggs or other dairy products. Watch for additives that contain the word "caseinate" — they are made from milk. Whey is also added to many processed foods.
- **SOUP STOCKS:** I've provided a recipe for homemade vegetable stock on page 59, but if you decide not to make your own, make sure the boxed vegetable stock you purchase is made only from plants.

PLANNING, SHOPPING AND PREPPING

So how do you become a meal prepper? The meal plans on pages 19–23 make it easy. Follow them and you'll have what you need for three meals a day, five days a week. On the remaining days, you can use up leftovers and go out to eat, if desired. Breakfasts are super-simple to make the night before or in the morning. Lunches come together very quickly and are packable for work or school, and you can make them the night before, the morning of or, for some, even on the prep day — whatever works best for you. Most of the dinners take only around 30 minutes to get on the table, thanks to your prep work.

The shopping lists and recipes are based on four servings per meal. If you are cooking for two, buy half as much of each ingredient and scale back the recipe by half. If you are dining solo, make half-batches and either freeze the second portion for another week or eat it later in the week, in place of another scheduled meal.

If you are new to prepping, you may want to start small. Each week includes optional prep that you can include or skip, depending on how much time you have on your prep day. You can either sub in store-bought ingredients (such as broth or mayonnaise) or simply prepare an item later in the week, as you need it.

GETTING READY TO PREP

IT MAY TAKE a little bit of time to set up your schedule and get ready for your prep day. Choose a day for the shopping and prep work. You can shop the day before you prep, to make the prep day shorter, but the bonus of shopping in the morning of your prep day is that you don't have to put things away — just prep them right out of the bag!

Before the shop day, make sure you have enough containers to hold all your prepped food and clean out your pantry, fridge and freezer. Clear room in your refrigerator for a whole week's worth of meal components. Ditch the junk food and anything that will get in the way of your new plan. You need the space for your healthy vegan staples.

Once your space is cleared and you have stocked up with containers as needed, take an inventory of what pantry supplies you already have, review the meal plan for the coming week, make a list and go shopping for anything you're missing from the Pantry Staples list on pages 24–25, plus your supplies for Week 1 (page 26).

RESTOCK LIST

Many people find it helpful to keep a list of pantry items somewhere in the kitchen so that you can make a note when you use up a can of tomatoes or the last of the olive oil.

CONTAINERS

Unless you already have a pretty extensive collection of containers, you may need to make a trip to a store that carries a good selection of storage options. The list below will take care of the minimum for prep and lunches, but you might want to have a few more containers on hand just in case. If you can't find good containers in your neighborhood, you can get anything on the internet — just plan accordingly.

GLASS VERSUS PLASTIC

In the effort to conserve, some of us save old yogurt tubs and the like to use for food storage. While this is certainly frugal, it's really not the best way to store food. Disposable tubs will leach chemicals into your food, so it's best to recycle them.

There are brands of plastic food storage containers that pledge that they contain no BPA (bisphenol A), but they may still contain BPS (bisphenol S) and phthalates. All of these are toxins that, for many years, have been routinely added to the plastics used for food containers. When it comes to your health, glass containers are safer. It's especially important to use nonreactive, inert materials like glass to hold hot or acidic foods, such as tomato sauce.

When packing your lunch, you may find that glass containers are a little heavy. It's considered pretty safe to put something like a cold sandwich in a plastic bag or wrap, as long as no acidic ingredients come in contact with the plastic and you don't heat it in the wrapper.

If you don't want to invest quite as much in containers, large, flat plastic storage tubs are probably safe for storing cooled baked goods, like muffins, bars and cupcakes, as long as you line the bottom with a piece of parchment paper.

TEMPERED GLASS CONTAINERS AND JARS

Tempered glass is the best choice because it is safe in the oven, microwave and freezer. Look for glass containers with durable lids. Glasslock, Pyrex and other brands that double as baking dishes will withstand the rigors of a normal kitchen.

If you got into the mason jar trend a few years back, you are in luck. Beans, grains, soups, salad dressings and more can be stored and toted in your reusable jars. You'll be happier and will have an easier time if you get widemouthed jars. To use the smaller, standard-mouth jars, you might need a jar funnel, to help you get that ladleful of spaghetti sauce or soup into the jar. Keep some extra lids on hand; the standard canning lids last for only so long, and can rust and discolor with time. They are cheap and easy to replace, so don't stick with lids that are funky.

STAINLESS STEEL

The bento box and the tiffin are the models for most stainless steel food containers. Stainless steel is nonreactive, so you can put acidic foods in it or even pop it in a warm oven. You can't microwave it, but you can always transfer the food to a plate if you want to warm it up in the microwave at work. Stainless steel is lighter than glass and won't crack or break if you drop it.

Some stainless steel baking pans, made for cakes or lasagna, come with reusable lids. These can be great for nontoxic food storage, and their rectangular shape makes them space-savers in the refrigerator.

PLASTIC BAGS AND ALTERNATIVES

There are times when toting glass or metal is too heavy and bulky. Environmentally conscious lunch eaters have been busy creating alternatives to plastic bags. Waxed fabric, linen, hemp, silicone and other materials are being made into reusable wraps, bags and containers that can be cleaned and used hundreds of times, so look for them in your natural foods store or online.

If you want to use plastic, zip-top bags can be used to tote sandwiches and other nonacidic foods. If you place two paper towels in the baggie and tuck your sandwich, salad greens or uncooked vegetables between them, you will minimize contact with the plastic. You can turn the bags inside out and handwash them, then air-dry and reuse them.

WAXED PAPER AND PARCHMENT PAPER

Waxed paper and parchment paper don't leach chemicals into your food and have less impact on the environment than plastic wrap. Both will biodegrade in a landfill, whereas plastics last for many years. Look for compostable sandwich bags and wrappers, which are already folded, or play around with folding and tucking your paper wraps so you don't need plastic bags.

YOUR CONTAINER NEEDS

Your storage needs will be a bit different each week, but in general, you'll need:

PREP CONTAINERS

- One 10-cup (2.5 L) container, or smaller containers that add up to 10 cups (2.5 L)
- Six 8-cup (2 L) containers
- Three 3-cup (750 mL) containers
- Four 1-pint (500 mL) jars or 2-cup (500 mL) containers
- Two 1-cup (250 mL) containers
- A large container for muffins and cupcakes
- More large containers for desserts and snacks

LUNCH CONTAINERS

- Four 4-cup (1 L) containers
- Four 3-cup (750 mL) containers
- Four 2-cup (500 mL) containers
- Four 1-cup (250 mL) containers
- Four ½-cup (125 mL) containers
- Four small containers for salad dressings and condiments

If you are prepping for one or two people instead of four, buy prep containers that are half the size listed here, and buy half as many of the lunch containers. If you decide to prep some of your lunches ahead of time, you'll need enough containers for several days of lunches, plus enough room in your fridge.

EQUIPMENT

You don't need to be a whiz in the kitchen to be a meal prepper, or to have a professional setup. All you need are a few basics that most home cooks already have:

- Large cutting board
- 8-inch (20 cm) chef's knife and a steel or sharpener to keep it honed
- 3½-inch (9 cm) paring knife
- Two to four 18- by 13-inch (46 by 33 cm) rimmed baking sheets
- 13- by 9-inch (33 by 23 cm) rectangular baking pan
- 8-inch (20 cm) square baking pan
- 8-cup (2 L) baking dish or casserole dish with a lid
- 2 wire cooling racks
- 6-quart (6 L) stockpot
- 4-quart (4 L) stockpot
- 2-quart (2 L) saucepan with lid
- 1-quart (1 L) saucepan with lid
- 12-inch (30 cm) skillet
- Small skillet for making individual scrambles
- Large, medium and small mixing bowls
- A few sturdy wooden or metal spoons
- Spatulas, both silicone and the metal "hamburger turner" type
- Blender
- Mini chopper or immersion blender
- A food processor is very helpful but not required; if you don't have one, you'll need a box grater or another type of grater for cabbage and carrots
- Parchment paper for lining pans
- Plenty of kitchen towels
- Labeling tape (masking tape or painter's tape work well and come in various colors) and a permanent marker for labeling your containers

THE FIVE-WEEK MEAL PLAN

THESE MEAL PLANS provide a total of at least 50 grams of protein per day. If you need more protein (see page 8), add a glass of nondairy milk (soy milk is the highest in protein) to your meal, eat high-protein snacks (such as nuts, seeds, hummus or soy yogurt) in between meals, or indulge in a healthy dessert or sweet snack, such as the ones on pages 170–185.

OPTIONAL SWEETS AND TREATS

Know yourself. Do you need some sweets and treats? Plan to make the optional vegan treats on your prep day (see the prep plans on pages 31–36), or make sure you have some healthy vegan snacks, like dried fruit, nuts, dark chocolate and frozen bananas, on hand.

week 1

DAY 1

BREAKFAST: Quinoa Tofu Scramble

LUNCH: Roasted Vegetable and Chickpea Pan Bagnat

DINNER: Avocado Quesadillas with Raspberry Salsa

Everyday Green Salad with Balsamic Vinaigrette

DAY 2

BREAKFAST: Maple Granola with Almonds and Raisins

LUNCH: Quinoa Bowls with Kale and Edamame

DINNER: Roasted Vegetable Chickpea Penne with Sun-Dried Tomato Pesto

Arugula Salad with Balsamic Vinaigrette

DAY 3

BREAKFAST: Jars of Oats with Berries and Coconut Yogurt

LUNCH: Sweet Potato Hummus with Pitas and Cucumbers

DINNER: Quinoa Corn Chowder

Everyday Green Salad with Sesame-Miso Garlic Dressing

DAY 4

BREAKFAST: Sweet Potato Pie Skin-Saver Smoothies

LUNCH: Quinoa Tabbouleh with Olives

DINNER: Curried Chickpeas and Kale

Quinoa (½ cup/125 mL per serving)

Roasted Broccoli and Onion (1 cup/250 mL per serving)

DAY 5

BREAKFAST: Quinoa and Mango Breakfast Bowls

LUNCH: Big Wraps with Carrots, Edamame and Spinach

DINNER: Roasted Cauliflower and Walnut Burritos with Cherry Tomato Salsa

week 2

DAY 1

BREAKFAST: Cranberry Muesli with Pecans

LUNCH: Blueberry Black Rice Salad with Radishes and Mint

Unsweetened plain soy milk (1 cup/250 mL per serving)

DINNER: Thai Red Curry Eggplant Stew with Tofu and Black Rice

Whole-Grain Biscuits (2 per serving)

DAY 2

BREAKFAST: Lemon Pecan Muffins with Apricot Cashew Spread (2 per serving)

LUNCH: Tempeh Banh Mi

DINNER: Creamy Kale Soup with Almonds

Pizza Bread

DAY 3

BREAKFAST: Green Smoothies with Turmeric

Rye toast with almond butter (1 slice toast and $1\frac{1}{2}$ tbsp/ 22 mL almond butter per serving)

LUNCH: Tofu Sandwiches with Tomatoes, Lettuce and Avocado

DINNER: Spaghetti with Cauliflower and Chickpeas

Everyday Green Salad with Basil Vinaigrette

DAY 4

BREAKFAST: Sweet Potato Chickpea Cakes (2 per serving)

LUNCH: Korean Mock Duck Lettuce Wraps with Black Rice

DINNER: Tempeh Pasta Salad with Tomato and Avocado

DAY 5

BREAKFAST: Peanut Butter and Chocolate Smoothies

LUNCH: Tempeh Reubens on Rye

Arugula Salad with Basil Vinaigrette

DINNER: Sweet Potato Soup with Spinach

Whole-Grain Biscuits (2 per serving)

Tomato Basil Salad

week 3

DAY 1

BREAKFAST: Breakfast Protein Cookies with Dates and Pistachios (3 per serving)

Unsweetened plain soy milk (1 cup/250 mL per serving)

LUNCH: Black Bean Nachos with Olives

DINNER: Roasted Carrot Soup with Barley and Pesto

Sweet Potato Cornbread (2 squares per serving)

DAY 2

BREAKFAST: Barley with Vanilla Apples and Spiced Sweet Potato

LUNCH: Shredded Veggie Salad with Pesto

Unsweetened plain soy milk (1 cup/250 mL per serving)

DINNER: Tofu Quinoa Burgers (1 per serving)

Asian Cucumber Salad

DAY 3

BREAKFAST: Cornbread Tofu Scramble

LUNCH: Chickpea Slaw Wraps with Cheesy Sauce

DINNER: Big Nutty Caesar Salad

Lemony Pesto Beets

DAY 4

BREAKFAST: Green Almond Protein Smoothies

Whole wheat toast with almond butter (1 slice toast and 1 tbsp/15 mL almond butter per serving)

LUNCH: Barley, Tofu Burger and Beet Bowls with Basil Vinaigrette

DINNER: Pesto Pasta with Broccoli and Carrots

Green Salad with Cashew Dressing

DAY 5

BREAKFAST: Sweet Potato Spice Smoothie Bowls with Sesame Quinoa

LUNCH: Avocado Goddess Salad with Edamame

DINNER: "Mac and Cheese" with a Nutty Crunch Topping

Crispy Kale with Lemon

week 4

DAY 1

BREAKFAST: Peach Power Smoothies

Whole wheat toast with peanut butter (1 slice toast and 1 tbsp/15 mL peanut butter per serving)

LUNCH: Chile-Lime Black Bean Hummus with Chips and Salsa

DINNER: Creamy Squash Soup with Farro and Sage

Whole-Grain Biscuits (2 per serving)

Unsweetened plain soy milk (1 cup/250 mL per serving)

DAY 2

BREAKFAST: Green Papaya Smoothies

Whole wheat toast with peanut butter (1 slice toast and 1 tbsp/15 mL peanut butter per serving)

LUNCH: Farro and Kimchi Bowls with Kale and Sesame Dressing

DINNER: Black Bean and Sweet Potato Curry

Whole wheat flatbreads (1 per serving)

Broccolini with Peanuts

DAY 3

BREAKFAST: Blueberry Breakfast Squares (2 per serving)

Almonds (12 per serving)

Unsweetened plain soy milk (1 cup/250 mL per serving)

LUNCH: Black Bean Burritos with Squash and Cilantro Farro

DINNER: Spaghetti with Broccolini and Cherry Tomatoes

Garlic Toast

Green Salad with Cashew Dressing

DAY 4

BREAKFAST: Prep-Ahead Steel-Cut Oats with Pears and Spiced Squash

LUNCH: Farro Salad with Apricots, Carrot and Spinach

8-inch (20 cm) whole wheat pitas (1 per serving)

DINNER: Black Bean and Squash Chili with Dumplings

Unsweetened plain soy milk (1 cup/250 mL per serving)

DAY 5

BREAKFAST: Farro, Banana and Peanut Butter Bowls

LUNCH: Squash and Black Bean Roll-Ups with Spinach

Unsweetened plain soy milk (1 cup/250 mL per serving)

DINNER: Thai Yellow Curry Tofu with Noodles

Everyday Green Salad with Sesame-Miso Garlic Dressing

week 5

DAY 1

BREAKFAST: Creamy Brown Rice Cereal with Dates and Pistachios

LUNCH: Tempeh Tacos with Mango Sriracha Sauce

DINNER: Mumbai Lentils and Kale

Roasted Broccoli (½ cup/ 125 mL per serving)

DAY 2

BREAKFAST: Granola and Soy Yogurt with Berries

Whole wheat toast with almond butter (1 slice toast and 1 tbsp/15 mL almond butter per serving)

LUNCH: Brown Rice Bowls with Roasted Carrots and Mock Duck

DINNER: Tempeh Meatloaf

Roasted Carrots (½ cup/ 125 mL per serving)

Everyday Green Salad with Balsamic Vinaigrette

DAY 3

BREAKFAST: Tofu Brown Rice Scramble

Whole wheat toast with tahini (1 slice toast and 1 tbsp/15 mL tahini per serving)

LUNCH: Sweet Potato and Mumbai Lentils with Cucumber Raita

DINNER: Sushi Bowls with Avocado, Edamame, Pickled Ginger and Cabbage

Quick Miso Soup

DAY 4

BREAKFAST: Blueberry Whole-Grain Pancakes with Maple and Pecans (2 per serving)

Unsweetened plain soy milk (1 cup/250 mL per serving)

LUNCH: Tempeh, Brown Rice and Roasted Veggie Wraps

DINNER: Jamaican Curried Beans and Greens

Medium-Grain Brown Rice (½ cup/125 mL per serving)

Tropical Fruit Salad with Mint

DAY 5

BREAKFAST: Sweet Potato Bowls with Greens and Maple Peanut Sauce

LUNCH: Meatloaf Sandwiches with Lettuce and Tomato

DINNER: Moroccan Chickpeas over Couscous with Roasted Broccoli

SHOPPING LISTS

The lists that follow contain all of the ingredients you'll need to prepare the meals in this book. First, make sure you are stocked up on pantry staples, then shop for each week just before your prep day. Before you shop, review all of the recipes for the coming week in case you want to add optional ingredients (which are otherwise not included in the lists) or to make a suggested substitution or variation. Decide whether you want to make any desserts or snacks for the week, too, and add those ingredients to your list as needed.

In the weekly shopping lists, amounts in parentheses after a food item are the total quantities that will be used in recipes that week; use leftovers for snacks, to make meals on your two "free" days each week, or to make bonus prep items such as veggie stock or bread crumbs. In some cases, you may be able to roll ingredients with a long shelf life over to the next week.

CHECK YOUR SUPPLIES

Before your weekly shopping trip, look through your pantry staples to see if you're running low on anything (or better yet, add items to a restock list as you notice them running low), particularly items that will be used in a number of recipes or in large amounts in the upcoming week. Also check to see if you have leftover items (such as dried beans, frozen corn, gingerroot or garlic) from the previous week that are still good and can carry over into the coming week.

pantry staples

CANNED GOODS
Coconut milk

Black beans

Red kidney beans

Chickpeas

Diced tomatoes

Tomato purée

Tomato paste

NUTS, SEEDS AND BUTTERS
Sliced almonds

Slivered almonds

Whole almonds

Raw cashews

Roasted cashews

Unsalted roasted peanuts

Pecan halves

Pine nuts

Pistachios

Walnut halves

Chia seeds

Golden flax seeds

Ground flax seeds (flaxseed meal)

Hemp seeds

Green pumpkin seeds (pepitas)

Sesame seeds

Raw sunflower seeds

Roasted sunflower seeds

Almond butter

Natural peanut butter (smooth or crunchy)

Tahini

DRIED FRUIT
Apricots

Cranberries

Dates

Raisins

OILS AND VINEGARS

Canola oil

Coconut oil

Extra virgin olive oil

Olive oil (regular or virgin)

Toasted (dark) sesame oil

Apple cider vinegar

Balsamic vinegar

Red wine vinegar

Rice vinegar (unseasoned)

White wine vinegar

CONDIMENTS AND FLAVORINGS

Hot pepper sauce

Cholula hot sauce

Gochujang

Sriracha

Ketchup

Dijon mustard

Vegan mayonnaise (unless you make your own)

Tamari

Thai red curry paste

Thai yellow curry paste

Roasted red peppers

Kalamata olives

Black olive paste (vegan tapenade)

Minced sweet pickle or relish

Pickled ginger slices

White miso

Red miso

Almond extract

Vanilla extract

Unsweetened cocoa powder

Nutritional yeast

GRAINS, FLOURS, STARCHES AND LEAVENERS

Large-flake (old-fashioned) rolled oats

Steel-cut oats

Panko

Unbleached all-purpose flour

Whole wheat pastry flour

White whole wheat flour (if available)

Medium-grind cornmeal

Arrowroot starch

Baking powder

Baking soda

SWEETENERS

Granulated sugar

Light brown sugar

Maple syrup

SPICES AND DRIED HERBS

Ground allspice

Basil

Bay leaves

Black mustard seeds

Black peppercorns (or ground pepper)

Cayenne pepper

Chili powder

Chipotle chile powder

Ground cinnamon

Ground coriander

Cumin seeds (whole)

Ground cumin

Dillweed

Granulated garlic

Hot pepper flakes

Oregano

Smoked paprika

Sweet paprika

Pumpkin pie spice

Sage

Salt

Thyme

Ground turmeric

NONDAIRY MILK AND YOGURT

Soy milk and yogurt offer the most protein of all the nondairy options, but any nondairy milk or yogurt can be substituted in the recipes in this book, though you may want to find other ways to increase the protein in the meal. Make sure to choose unsweetened plain soy milk and yogurt unless otherwise specified.

week 1

PRODUCE

VEGETABLES
1½ lbs (750 g) broccoli

2¼ lbs (1.125 kg) cauliflower

2 medium cucumbers

2 small cucumbers

2 tomatoes

2 cups (500 mL) cherry tomatoes

1 large red bell pepper

1 medium red bell pepper

1 green bell pepper

1 jalapeño pepper

1 gingerroot (for 2 tbsp/30 mL sliced)

2 heads garlic (or 13 cloves)

3 onions

1 red onion

1 large shallot (for ¼ cup/60 mL)

6 green onions

3 large carrots

6 oz (175 g) yellow-fleshed potatoes

1 lb (500 g) sweet potatoes

GREENS
10 oz (300 g) salad greens

4 oz (125 g) baby arugula

6 oz (175 g) kale

4 oz (125 g) baby kale

6 oz (175 g) spinach

2 handfuls sprouts or pea shoots

FRESH HERBS
⅓ oz (10 g) basil

1 oz (28 g) cilantro

3 oz (85 g) mint

5½ oz (156 g) parsley

FRUIT
2 cups (500 mL) berries (fresh or frozen)

1½ cups (375 mL) raspberries

4 avocados

2 kiwifruits

2 Ataulfo mangos (or 2 cups/500 mL cubed mango)

5 lemons

1 lime

BREAD
Four 6-inch (15 cm) baguette pieces or hoagie buns

Eight 10-inch (25 cm) whole wheat tortillas

Eight 8-inch (20 cm) whole wheat tortillas

Four 8-inch (20 cm) whole wheat pitas

GROCERY
8 oz (250 g) dried whole wheat penne pasta

2½ lbs (1.25 kg) quinoa

1 lb (500 g) dried chickpeas

5 oz (150 g) dry-packed sun-dried tomatoes

2 cups (500 mL) ready-to-use no-salt-added vegetable broth (unless using homemade stock)

REFRIGERATED
7 cups (1.75 L) unsweetened plain soy milk

2 cups (500 mL) vanilla-flavored soy milk (or additional plain soy milk)

4 cups (1 L) plain soy yogurt

2 cups (500 mL) coconut milk yogurt

12 oz (375 g) water-packed extra-firm tofu

FROZEN
20 oz (600 g) shelled edamame

10 oz (300 g) corn kernels

week 2

PRODUCE

VEGETABLES
22 oz (600 g) cauliflower

8 oz (250 g) eggplant

1 head celery (for 1 stalk)

1 medium cucumber

1 small cucumber

4 large tomatoes

2 medium tomatoes

1 red bell pepper

1 red Fresno chile pepper or jalapeño pepper

1 gingerroot (for 6 slices)

1 turmeric root (for 2 tbsp/30 mL slivered)

1 head garlic (or 6 cloves)

3 onions

1 red onion

2 small shallots

8 green onions

1 carrot

3 large red radishes

½ daikon radish (ask your grocer to cut one in half)

2½ lbs (1.25 kg) sweet potatoes

GREENS
2 heads Bibb or butter lettuce

1 small head romaine lettuce

1 lb (500 g) kale

14 oz (425 g) spinach

4 oz (125 g) baby spinach

1 handful sprouts or pea shoots

FRESH HERBS
2¼ oz (64 g) basil

2 sprigs cilantro

3 oz (85 g) mint

5¾ oz (163 g) parsley

5 sprigs rosemary

4 sprigs thyme

FRUIT
4 cups (1 L) cubed pineapple

1½ cups (375 mL) blueberries

2 avocados

2 bananas

1 lemon

1 lime

BREAD
1 loaf rye bread (for 12 slices)

1 loaf whole wheat bread (for ½ cup/125 mL fresh bread crumbs)

3 large white baguettes

GROCERY
Two 10-oz (284 g) cans mock duck

8 oz (250 g) dried whole wheat spaghetti

4 oz (125 g) dried whole wheat rotini pasta

18 oz (550 g) black rice

7 oz (200 g) dried chickpeas

3 cups (750 mL) ready-to-use vegetable broth (unless using homemade stock)

¼ cup (60 mL) red wine

REFRIGERATED
1½ cups (375 mL) unsweetened apple juice

1 cup (250 mL) cranberry juice

14¼ cups (3.55 L) unsweetened plain soy milk

2 cups (500 mL) unsweetened plain almond milk

3 cups (750 mL) plain soy yogurt

2 cups (500 mL) vanilla-flavored soy yogurt

32 oz (1 kg) tempeh

36 oz (1.125 kg) water-packed extra-firm tofu

1½ cups (375 mL) kimchi

1½ cups (375 mL) sauerkraut

week 3

PRODUCE

VEGETABLES
8 oz (250 g) broccoli florets

1 head cauliflower

5 small cucumbers (about 1 1/4 lbs/625 g total)

2 tomatoes

1 cup (250 mL) cherry tomatoes

1/2 cup (125 mL) grape tomatoes

2 heads garlic (or 13 cloves)

2 onions

2 small shallots

7 green onions

3 1/2 lbs (1.75 kg) carrots

2 1/2 lbs (1.25 kg) beets

1 3/4 lbs (875 g) sweet potatoes

GREENS
4 oz (125 g) baby kale mix or other salad greens

1 head romaine lettuce

5 oz (150 g) baby romaine lettuce

3 oz (90 g) arugula

34 oz (1.06 kg) cabbage

1 lb (500 g) kale

8 oz (250 g) spinach

2 oz (60 g) broccoli sprouts

FRESH HERBS
6 oz (170 g) basil

2 3/4 oz (78 g) parsley

FRUIT
4 Granny Smith apples

4 medium apples

2 avocados

2 large bananas

2 lemons

2 limes

BREAD
1 loaf whole wheat bread (for 8 slices)

Four 10-inch (25 cm) whole wheat tortillas

4 whole wheat hamburger buns

GROCERY
8 oz (250 g) dried whole wheat rotini pasta

8 oz (250 g) dried whole wheat macaroni

20 oz (600 g) hulled, pot or pearl barley

8 oz (250 g) quinoa

4 oz (125 g) tortilla chips

1 cup (250 mL) ready-to-use vegetable broth (unless using homemade stock)

1/2 cup (125 mL) dry white wine

REFRIGERATED
15 cups (3.75 L) unsweetened plain soy milk

4 cups (1 L) plain soy yogurt

28 oz (875 g) water-packed extra-firm tofu

6 oz (175 g) silken tofu

FROZEN
3 oz (85 g) corn kernels

21 oz (596 g) strawberries

6 oz (170 g) shelled edamame

week 4

PRODUCE

VEGETABLES

7½ lbs (3.75 kg) kabocha or red kuri squash

1 lb (500 g) broccolini

2 small cucumbers

2 large tomatoes

2 medium tomatoes

1 cup (250 mL) cherry tomatoes

3 red bell peppers

1 green bell pepper

1 large jalapeño pepper

1 medium jalapeño pepper

4 oz (125 g) shiitake mushrooms

1 gingerroot (for 3 tbsp/45 mL chopped)

2 heads garlic (or 13 cloves)

5 onions

6 green onions

2 carrots

18 oz (550 g) sweet potato

GREENS

4 to 5 oz (125 to 150 g) salad greens

4 oz (125 g) baby kale mix or other salad greens

8 oz (250 g) kale

1 lb (500 g) spinach

1 handful sprouts or pea shoots

FRESH HERBS

5½ oz (156 g) cilantro

6¾ oz (192 g) parsley

FRUIT

1 cup (250 mL) blueberries

2 large pears

4 large bananas

2 medium bananas

1 lemon

5 limes

BREAD

1 loaf whole wheat bread (for 8 slices)

1 large white baguette

Eight 10-inch (25 cm) whole wheat tortillas

Four 8-inch (20 cm) whole wheat pitas

4 whole wheat flatbreads

GROCERY

8 oz (250 g) dried whole wheat spaghetti

8 oz (250 g) flat rice noodles

29 oz (824 g) farro

1½ lbs (682 g) dried black beans

4 oz (125 g) tortilla chips

3¼ cups (800 mL) ready-to-use vegetable broth (unless using homemade stock)

1 jar strawberry jam (for 2 tbsp/30 mL)

REFRIGERATED

25 cups (6.25 L) unsweetened plain soy milk

2 cups (500 mL) plain soy yogurt

12 oz (375 g) water-packed extra-firm tofu

1 cup (250 mL) guacamole (or 1 avocado)

1½ cups (375 mL) kimchi

FROZEN

20 oz (568 g) peach slices

16 oz (454 g) papaya chunks

week 5

PRODUCE

VEGETABLES

1 lb (500 g) broccoli

8 oz (250 g) snow peas

1 head celery

1 medium cucumber

2 small cucumbers

2 tomatoes

2 cups (500 mL) grape tomatoes

1 red bell pepper

4 jalapeño peppers

1 gingerroot (for 3 tbsp/45 mL chopped/grated)

1 turmeric root (for 1 slice)

2 heads garlic (or 16 cloves)

6 onions

8 green onions

$3\frac{1}{2}$ lbs (1.75 kg) carrots

$2\frac{1}{2}$ lbs (1.25 kg) sweet potatoes

GREENS

5 oz (150 g) salad greens

1 lb (500 g) red cabbage

$3\frac{1}{2}$ lbs (1.75 kg) kale

2 oz (60 g) spinach

4 oz (125 g) baby spinach

1 handful sprouts or pea shoots

FRESH HERBS

$2\frac{3}{4}$ oz (78 g) mint

$1\frac{1}{2}$ oz (57 g) parsley

FRUIT

2 cups (500 mL) berries

$\frac{1}{2}$ cup (125 mL) blueberries

4 avocados

1 large mango

2 medium mangos

3 lemons

1 lime

BREAD

1 large loaf whole wheat bread (for 19 slices)

8 hard taco shells or 6-inch (15 cm) corn tortillas

4 whole wheat flatbreads

Four 10-inch (25 cm) whole wheat tortillas

GROCERY

Two 10-oz (284 g) cans mock duck

38 oz (1.08 g) medium-grain brown rice

6 oz (170 g) whole wheat couscous

7 oz (200 g) dried red lentils

$10\frac{1}{2}$ cups (2.625 L) ready-to-use reduced-sodium vegetable broth (unless using homemade stock)

REFRIGERATED

$1\frac{3}{4}$ cups (425 mL) unsweetened apple juice

$6\frac{1}{2}$ cups (1.625 L) unsweetened plain soy milk

$2\frac{1}{2}$ cups (625 mL) plain soy yogurt

64 oz (2 kg) tempeh

12 oz (375 g) water-packed extra-firm tofu

FROZEN

8 oz (224 g) shelled edamame

WEEKLY PREP PLANS

THE NIGHT BEFORE your prep day, have a look at the prep plan for the coming week. You may need to do a little bit of pre-prep, such as soaking beans or marinating tofu or tempeh overnight, so you'll want to get that started before you head to bed.

Get set for your prep day by reviewing the recipes, clearing some counter space and setting out your cutting board, knives and bowls, as well as the pots and other equipment you'll need. If everything is ready to go in advance, it will save you some time and confusion when you actually start prepping.

As you prep, you will have food cooking both in the oven and on the stove, and you will be able to work on other types of prep at the same time. While the chickpeas cook or the granola bakes, you will have blocks of time in which to chop vegetables or make dressing. You will also have some periods of down time in which you can relax or get some other chores done.

The total time estimates in the plans below are approximate and are given so that you have an idea of how much time to set aside for your prep. It may take longer at the beginning, but as you become more experienced, you'll get faster and be able to finish in the estimated time.

Each prep day also includes some optional prep, which you can add to your to-do list if you have extra time on your hands (and extra room in your fridge). If you have a sweet tooth, be sure to make one or more of the desserts. These vegan treats are sure to win over your friends and family — even the skeptics.

As you complete each food item, let it cool, pack it up and store it as directed. If there are no specific storage details in the prep pan, simply follow the instructions in the recipe.

CLEAN AS YOU GO

Have a stack of clean kitchen towels, a cooling rack, and a spot for draining clean dishes as you go. Professional cooks learn early that you clean as you go, and it's a good habit to establish. As you finish with a pot, pan or bowl, wash it by hand and let it air-dry, or load it in the dishwasher.

week 1

THE NIGHT BEFORE PREP DAY

Soak 2½ cups (625 mL) dried chickpeas (about 1 lb/500 g) overnight as directed in step 1 on page 55. (Alternatively, starting earlier in the day, soak them for at least 6 hours and cook them in a slow cooker on Low overnight.)

PREP DAY

1. Unless you cooked the chickpeas overnight, start cooking them now as directed on page 55. Freeze the aquafaba when you're done, as you won't need it this week. **10 MINUTES TO 4 HOURS, DEPENDING ON COOKING METHOD**
2. Preheat oven to 400°F (200°C). Bake 1 lb (500 g) sweet potatoes as directed on page 45. **40 TO 60 MINUTES, DEPENDING ON SIZE OF SWEET POTATOES**
3. Meanwhile, prepare 2¼ lbs (1.125 kg) cauliflower as described in step 1 on page 48 and prepare broccoli and onion as described in step 1 on page 47.
4. Roast cauliflower. **30 MINUTES**
5. Meanwhile, prepare Sesame-Miso Garlic Dressing as directed on page 163 and Balsamic Vinaigrette as directed on page 161.
6. Roast broccoli and onion. **20 MINUTES**
7. Meanwhile, prepare Maple Granola with Almonds and Raisins as directed in steps 1 and 2 on page 73.
8. Reduce oven temperature to 300°F (150°C). Bake granola. **1 HOUR**
9. Meanwhile, cook quinoa as directed on page 51. Put 5 oz (150 g) dry-packed sun-dried tomatoes in a bowl of water to soak, then cover tightly and refrigerate for use over the week.
10. Prepare Jars of Oats with Berries and Coconut Yogurt as directed on page 74.

OPTIONAL PREP

- Homemade Veggie Stock (page 59) if you want to use homemade stock in your chowder
- Cashew Parmesan (page 69) if you want it handy to sprinkle on dishes
- Roasted Vegetable and Chickpea Pan Bagnat (page 100) for Day 1 lunch
- Sweet Potato Hummus (page 102) for Day 3 lunch
- Quinoa Corn Chowder (page 130) for Day 3 dinner
- Desserts and snacks of your choice (pages 170–185)

week 2

THE NIGHT BEFORE PREP DAY

1. Soak 1 cup (250 mL) dried chickpeas overnight as directed in step 1 on page 55. (Alternatively, starting earlier in the day, soak them for at least 6 hours and cook them in a slow cooker on Low overnight.)
2. Marinate tofu for Baked Marinated Tofu as directed in steps 1 and 2 on page 56.
3. Marinate tempeh for Baked Marinated Tempeh as directed in steps 1 and 2 on page 57.
4. Soak cashews for the Apricot Cashew Spread as directed on page 79.

PREP DAY

1. Unless you cooked the chickpeas overnight, start cooking them now as directed on page 55. If making the optional Aquafaba Mayo (see below), keep out $\frac{1}{4}$ cup (60 mL) aquafaba and freeze the rest. 10 MINUTES TO 4 HOURS, DEPENDING ON COOKING METHOD
2. Preheat oven to 400°F (200°C). Bake tofu as directed on page 56. Store 12 slices in the refrigerator and freeze the rest. 40 MINUTES
3. Meanwhile, cook black rice as directed on page 52, prepare Whole-Grain Baking Mix as directed on page 41, and prepare Basil Vinaigrette as directed on page 162.
4. Bake tempeh as directed on page 57. You will use most of it up over the week, so store it all in the refrigerator and enjoy the leftover 8 slices for snacks. 25 MINUTES
5. Meanwhile, chop vegetables for Veggie Spaghetti Sauce (page 61) and prepare 1 lb 6 oz (600 g) cauliflower as described in step 1 on page 48.
6. Bake $2\frac{1}{2}$ lbs (1.25 kg) sweet potatoes as directed on page 45. 40 TO 60 MINUTES
7. Meanwhile, cook the spaghetti sauce as directed on page 61. Store 1 cup (250 mL) in the fridge and 3 cups (750 mL) in the freezer.
8. Start soaking apricots for the Apricot Cashew Spread as directed on page 79.
9. Roast cauliflower. 30 MINUTES
10. Meanwhile, prepare batter for Lemon Pecan Muffins as directed in steps 1 to 4 on page 78.
11. Reduce oven temperature to 375°F (190°C) and bake muffins. 25 TO 30 MINUTES
12. Meanwhile, prepare Apricot Cashew Spread as directed on page 79 and prepare Cranberry Muesli as directed in step 1 on page 77.
13. Reduce oven temperature to 300°F (150°C) and prepare Cashew Parmesan as directed on page 69. You will have enough for Weeks 2 and 3. 15 MINUTES

OPTIONAL PREP

- Homemade Veggie Stock (page 59) if you didn't make it in Week 1 and you want to use homemade stock in your soups
- Aquafaba Mayo (page 68) if desired for sandwiches
- Blueberry Black Rice Salad with Radishes and Mint (page 105) for Day 1 lunch
- Creamy Kale Soup with Almonds (page 134) for Day 2 dinner
- Desserts and snacks of your choice (pages 170–185)

week 3

THE NIGHT BEFORE PREP DAY

Place 3 cups (750 mL) raw cashews in a large bowl and add enough cold water to cover. Soak overnight.

PREP DAY

1. Preheat oven to 400°F (200°C). Bake 1¾ lbs (875 g) sweet potatoes as directed on page 45. **40 TO 60 MINUTES, DEPENDING ON SIZE OF SWEET POTATOES**

2. Meanwhile, cook barley as directed on page 49, prepare Shredded Cabbage and Carrots as directed on page 44, and prepare beets as directed on page 46.

3. Roast beets. **40 TO 60 MINUTES, DEPENDING ON SIZE OF BEETS**

4. Meanwhile, cook 1¼ cups (300 mL) quinoa in 2 cups (500 mL) water as directed on page 51 and prepare 2½ lbs (1.25 kg) carrots as directed in step 1 on page 47.

5. Roast carrots. **30 MINUTES**

6. Meanwhile, drain cashews and use 2 cups (500 mL) to prepare a double batch of Creamy Cheesy Sauce as directed in steps 2 and 3 on page 62. Prepare batter for Sweet Potato Cornbread as directed in steps 1 to 3 on page 43.

7. Bake cornbread. **25 MINUTES**

8. Meanwhile, use the remaining cashews to prepare Creamy Cashew Dressing as directed in step 2 on page 164. Prepare dough for Breakfast Protein Cookies with Dates and Pistachios as directed in steps 1 to 4 on page 83.

9. Reduce oven temperature to 350°F (180°C). Bake cookies. **16 MINUTES**

10. Meanwhile, prepare Basil Pesto as directed on page 66.

11. Prepare Creamy Cauliflower Sauce as directed on page 63. **35 MINUTES**

12. Prepare Basil Vinaigrette as directed on page 162. **10 MINUTES**

OPTIONAL PREP

- Homemade Veggie Stock (page 59) if you don't have any in the freezer and you want to use homemade stock in your soup
- Black Bean Nachos with Olives (page 111) for Day 1 lunch
- Shredded Veggie Salad with Pesto (page 112) for Day 2 lunch
- Tofu Quinoa Burgers (page 139) for Day 2 dinner and Day 4 lunch
- Asian Cucumber Salad (page 158) for Day 2 dinner
- Lemony Pesto Beets (page 166) for Day 3 dinner
- Desserts and snacks of your choice (pages 170–185)

week 4

THE NIGHT BEFORE PREP DAY

1. Soak black beans overnight as directed in step 1 on page 54.
2. Soak cashews for Creamy Cashew Dressing as directed in step 1 on page 164.

PREP DAY

1. Preheat oven to 400°F (200°C). Bake 8 oz (250 g) sweet potatoes as directed on page 45. **40 TO 60 MINUTES, DEPENDING ON SIZE OF SWEET POTATOES**
2. Meanwhile, cook black beans as directed on page 54, prepare Tomato Cilantro Salsa as directed on page 65, and prepare kabocha or red kuri squash as directed in step 1 on page 48.
3. Roast squash. **40 MINUTES**
4. Meanwhile, cook farro as directed on page 50, prepare Whole-Grain Baking Mix as directed on page 41, prepare Sesame-Miso Garlic Dressing as directed on page 163, and prepare broccolini as directed in step 1 on page 47.
5. Roast broccolini. **15 MINUTES**
6. Meanwhile, prepare batter for Blueberry Breakfast Squares as directed in steps 1 to 5 on page 90.
7. Reduce oven temperature to 350°F (180°C) and bake breakfast squares. **30 MINUTES**
8. Meanwhile, drain cashews and prepare Creamy Cashew Dressing as directed in step 2 on page 164.
9. Reduce oven temperature to 300°F (150°C) and prepare Cashew Parmesan (using the optional granulated garlic) as directed on page 69. **15 MINUTES**

OPTIONAL PREP

- Homemade Veggie Stock (page 59) if you don't have any in the freezer and you want to use homemade stock in your meals
- Chile-Lime Black Bean Hummus (page 116) for Day 1 lunch
- Farro and Kimchi Bowls with Kale and Sesame Dressing (page 117) for Day 2 lunch
- Desserts and snacks of your choice (pages 170–185)

week 5

THE NIGHT BEFORE PREP DAY

Marinate tempeh for Baked Marinated Tempeh as directed in steps 1 and 2 on page 57.

PREP DAY

1. Preheat oven to 400°F (200°C). Bake 2½ lbs (1.25 kg) sweet potatoes as directed on page 45. **40 TO 60 MINUTES, DEPENDING ON SIZE OF SWEET POTATOES**

2. Meanwhile, cook medium-grain brown rice as directed on page 53, prepare 3 lbs (1.5 kg) carrots as directed in step 1 on page 47, and prepare broccoli as directed in step 1 on page 46.

3. Roast carrots. **30 MINUTES**

4. Meanwhile, prepare Quick Miso Soup as directed on page 60.

5. Roast broccoli. **20 MINUTES**

6. Meanwhile, prepare Smoky Tempeh Taco Meat as directed on page 58. Store half in the refrigerator for this week's meals and freeze the rest.

7. Bake tempeh as directed on page 57. Store 24 slices in the refrigerator and the rest in the freezer. **25 MINUTES**

8. Meanwhile, prepare Fruity Low-Fat Granola as directed in steps 1 and 2 on page 40.

9. Reduce oven temperature to 300°F (150°C). Bake granola. **1 HOUR**

10. Meanwhile, prepare Whole-Grain Baking Mix as directed on page 41, prepare Mango Sriracha Sauce as directed on page 64, and prepare Balsamic Vinaigrette as directed on page 161.

OPTIONAL PREP

- Homemade Veggie Stock (page 59) if you don't have any in the freezer and you want to use homemade stock in your meals
- Aquafaba Mayo (page 68) if you want to use homemade mayo on your wraps and sandwiches and in your sushi bowls
- Mumbai Lentils and Kale (page 149) for Day 1 dinner and Day 3 lunch
- Tempeh Meatloaf (page 150) for Day 2 dinner
- Tropical Fruit Salad with Mint (page 160) for Day 4 dinner
- Desserts and snacks of your choice (pages 170–185)

LET'S GET COOKING!

....

125 VEGAN RECIPES

In the chapters that follow, you will find everything you need to make five weeks' worth of quick, easy meals. First up are recipes for the staples that will carry you through the week, packed with plant-powered flavor. Next, you'll find crave-worthy breakfast, lunch and dinner recipes to transform your gold mine of prep into tasty meals for you and your family, along with salads and sides to accompany your meals, tantalizing desserts to finish them off, and even snacks for those between-meal munchies.

As a bonus, each of the lunch recipes includes a convenient packing strategy, making it easy for you to get lunches ready for work or school. If the neighborhood around your workplace isn't vegan-friendly, these lunches will make your dietary choices so much easier. You may even find your co-workers giving your lunch a longing look — remember, the best way to convince the rest of the world that vegan diets are great is to eat good food!

VEGAN STAPLES

FRUITY LOW-FAT GRANOLA

MIXING APPLE JUICE into the oats allows you to use just a little oil and still get a wonderful texture in your granola. A hint of apple flavor goes perfectly with dates, for a fruity start to your day.

MAKES ABOUT 8 CUPS (2 L) | **Preheat oven to 300°F (150°C)**

Baking sheet, lined with parchment paper

¾ cup (175 mL) packed brown sugar

½ cup (125 mL) unsweetened apple juice

2 tbsp (30 mL) canola oil

1 tsp (5 mL) vanilla extract

¼ cup (60 mL) ground flax seeds (flaxseed meal)

4 cups (1 L) large-flake (old-fashioned) rolled oats

1 cup (250 mL) walnut halves, coarsely chopped

½ tsp (2 mL) salt

1 cup (250 mL) dates, chopped

1. In a medium bowl, stir together brown sugar, apple juice, oil and vanilla. Stir in flax seeds and let stand for 5 minutes to thicken slightly.
2. In a large bowl, combine oats, walnuts and salt. Pour in apple juice mixture and stir well. Spread mixture on prepared baking sheet and flatten with a spatula into an even layer.
3. Bake in preheated oven for 20 minutes, then turn granola with a spatula and press flat. Repeat twice more, for a total baking time of 1 hour. The granola will be golden and toasted-looking, and form large clumps. Let cool completely on sheet on a wire rack.
4. Stir in dates, being careful not to break up the granola chunks, then transfer to an airtight container. Keeps for up to 2 weeks at room temperature.

tips

Other sweeteners, such as coconut or palm sugar, which are less refined, can be used in place of the brown sugar.

Pressing the granola flat on the pan after turning it will cause it to form nice chunks, which are fun to eat with your fingers.

WHOLE-GRAIN BAKING MIX

I GREW UP in a household with a box of biscuit mix on the shelf. I always knew that Mom was in a hurry to get a meal on the table when she reached for that box. Unlike that mix, this one is made from whole grains and has no strange additives. Use it to make Whole-Grain Biscuits (page 42), Blueberry Whole-Grain Pancakes with Maple and Pecans (page 96) or dumplings for your Black Bean and Squash Chili (page 146).

MAKES ABOUT 4½ CUPS (1.125 L)

2 cups (500 mL) whole wheat pastry flour

2 cups (500 mL) white whole wheat flour (or additional whole wheat pastry flour)

2 tbsp (30 mL) granulated sugar

4 tsp (20 mL) baking powder

1 tsp (5 mL) baking soda

1 tsp (5 mL) salt

¼ cup (60 mL) solid coconut oil (see tip)

1. In a large bowl, whisk together pastry flour, white whole wheat flour, sugar, baking powder, baking soda and salt until evenly combined.
2. Using the coarse holes on a box grater, shred coconut oil into flour mixture. Toss to coat, mixing with your hands and squeezing to coat some of the flour with oil but leaving the oil in small pieces.
3. Use immediately or transfer the mix to an airtight container and store in the refrigerator for up to 1 month or in the freezer for up to 6 months.

tips

To measure solid coconut oil, melt it by placing the jar in a bowl and pouring warm water into the bowl to come up the sides but not to the top of the jar. (Or take the lid off and microwave the jar on High for 1 minute.) Measure out the amount you need, then place the measuring cup in the freezer to solidify the oil again.

Because you're mixing in the coconut oil in advance, the baking mix must be kept in the refrigerator or freezer.

WHOLE-GRAIN BISCUITS

A SIMPLE BOWL of soup or salad blossoms into a delectable meal when you have a hot biscuit on the side. Once your baking mix is prepped, these biscuits can be done in a snap, ready to be dipped in, smeared with or filled with just about anything.

MAKES 8 BISCUITS | Preheat oven to 400°F (200°C)

Baking sheet, lined with parchment paper

1 tbsp (15 mL) apple cider vinegar

Unsweetened plain soy milk

2 cups (500 mL) Whole-Grain Baking Mix (page 41)

Whole wheat pastry flour

1. Add vinegar to a measuring cup and add enough milk to make $3/4$ cup (175 mL), stirring to combine; let stand for 5 minutes to thicken.

2. Place baking mix in a large bowl and, using a fork, stir in milk mixture until a stiff dough forms. Gather and squeeze dough gently just to incorporate all the flour.

3. On a floured counter, pat dough into a $3/4$-inch (2 cm) thick rectangle or disk. Cut into 8 squares or wedges and transfer to prepared baking sheet, spacing them at least 1 inch (2.5 cm) apart.

4. Bake in preheated oven for 12 minutes or until golden brown. Transfer pan to a wire rack and let cool. Serve biscuits warm or cooled completely, as desired.

tips

Don't overmix the dough, or it will make tough biscuits.

The biscuits are best served right away, but they keep, tightly covered, for up to 3 days.

SWEET POTATO CORNBREAD

I KNOW YOU don't have time to make slow bread. But quick bread? That is completely doable. I love putting sweet potato in the mix, because it makes for a lovely deep orange color and keeps the bread moist for days. In Week 3, use 2 squares to make the Cornbread Tofu Scramble (page 85), serve some alongside Roasted Carrot Soup with Barley and Pesto (page 138) and save the rest for snacks!

MAKES 16 SQUARES | Preheat oven to 350°F (180°C)

8-inch (20 cm) square baking dish, greased

1 cup (250 mL) unbleached all-purpose flour

¾ cup (175 mL) medium-grind cornmeal

1 tsp (5 mL) baking powder

1 tsp (5 mL) salt

½ tsp (2 mL) baking soda

¾ cup (175 mL) unsweetened plain soy milk

1 tbsp (15 mL) apple cider vinegar

½ cup (125 mL) mashed baked sweet potato (see page 45)

¼ cup (60 mL) canola oil

¼ cup (60 mL) pure maple syrup

1. In a large bowl, whisk together flour, cornmeal, baking powder, salt and baking soda.
2. In another bowl, whisk together milk and vinegar. Whisk in sweet potato, oil and maple syrup.
3. Stir the sweet potato mixture into the flour mixture until smooth. Scrape into prepared pan and smooth top.
4. Bake in preheated oven for 25 minutes or until a tester inserted in the center comes out clean. Let cool in dish on a wire rack for 10 minutes. Cut into squares in the dish and serve, and once cooled completely, wrap leftovers tightly in the pan. Alternatively, run a knife around dish to loosen bread, then invert onto the rack and let cool completely before cutting squares.
5. Store squares in an airtight container at room temperature for up to 4 days or in the freezer for up to 3 months.

tips

Medium-grind cornmeal, which is coarser than the standard fine cornmeal, gives this bread a toothsome crunch. Bob's Red Mill is a good brand, but you can use other kinds.

If you can find red or blue cornmeal, try it in this recipe for a burst of color.

SHREDDED CABBAGE AND CARROTS

THE CONFOUNDING THING about shopping for vegetables is figuring out how much to buy. Most of the time, you buy a cabbage and shave some off, then wrap the rest and stuff it in the back of the vegetable drawer. On your prep day for Week 3, you'll shred the entire cabbage and a few carrots for the whole week. If you have a food processor, the shredding and slicing blades make this job much faster than doing it by hand.

MAKES ABOUT 12 CUPS (3 L)

Food processor (optional)

2 lbs (1 kg) cabbage

4 large carrots

USING A FOOD PROCESSOR

1. Insert the slicing blade into the food processor, put the lid on and have the tamper ready.
2. Core cabbage and cut into vertical pieces that will fit into the feed tube. With the motor running, drop cabbage into the feed tube. Don't push down with the tamper unless the cabbage becomes lodged in the feed tube — the less pressure you put on the cabbage, the thinner the slices will be. Empty the food processor bowl into a large bowl as it becomes full.
3. Switch to the coarse shredding blade and shred carrots. Add to cabbage and mix to combine.

USING A KNIFE AND A GRATER

1. Core cabbage and cut into wedges, then sliver thinly. Place in a large bowl.
2. Using the large holes of a box grater or other grater, coarsely shred carrots. Add to cabbage and mix to combine.

tips

The cabbage will yield 8 cups (2 L) shredded, and the carrots will yield about 4 cups (1 L) shredded.

The shredded vegetable mixture can be stored in airtight containers in the refrigerator for up to 1 week.

BAKED SWEET POTATO

A SIMPLE BAKED sweet potato is one of the most versatile prep-ahead items. Once you have a cache of tender, creamy sweet potato, you are ready to make soups, bake treats, or stir it into warm grains for breakfast. Sweet potatoes are both delicious and exceptionally nutritious, with loads of vitamins A and C and a host of other good things.

PREHEAT OVEN TO 400°F (200°C)

Baking sheet

Sweet potato(es) (see tip)

1. Place sweet potato(es) on baking sheet and pierce the skin on top of each potato once with a paring knife to vent steam as they cook. Roast in preheated oven for 40 to 60 minutes (depending on size of sweet potatoes) or until very soft when pierced with a paring knife. Let cool completely on pan on a wire rack.
2. Strip off sweet potato skins. Transfer to airtight containers and store in the refrigerator for up to 1 week or in the freezer for up to 3 months (thaw overnight in the refrigerator before use). When ready to use, mash, slice or chop sweet potato as directed in your recipe.

tips

For Week 1, you will need 1 lb (500 g) of sweet potatoes; for Week 2, you will need 2½ lbs (1.25 kg); for Week 3, you will need 1¾ lbs (875 g); for Week 4, you will need 8 oz (250 g); for Week 5, you will need 2½ lbs (1.25 kg).

One pound (500 g) of sweet potatoes makes about 2 cups (500 mL) mashed or about 3½ cups (875 mL) chopped.

ROASTED VEGETABLES

WHY ROAST? ROASTING vegetables removes some of the water from their cells, condensing them and making them intensely flavorful. The heat also caramelizes the naturally occurring sugars, making them a little sweeter.

Don't be alarmed when you're purchasing whole vegetables that will make a big pile of chopped — they shrink. Depending on the vegetable and cooking time, they'll lose up to a quarter or a third of their weight while in the oven. This makes them a fantastic prep-ahead item, providing you with delicious, ready-to-eat vegetables for the week in a space-saving package. Your prep plan will set you up with the roasted vegetables you need to make the recipes for that week, but you can always make more, if needed. Once you get the hang of this, you'll be roasting every week, like a pro.

On your prep day, a 400°F (200°C) oven is the best universal temperature for all the vegetables you'll be roasting. Once they are done, you can turn the heat down to make your granola, muffins or desserts.

Aside from the winter squash, all of the vegetables are roasted with a drizzle of olive oil. If you don't want to use oil, you can cover the pan tightly with foil instead. The vegetables will be softer and moister; if you want some browning, uncover the pan and roast on the top rack of the oven for 5 to 10 minutes.

ROASTED BEETS
(FOR WEEK 3)

Preheat oven to 400°F (200°C)
11- by 9-inch (28 by 23 cm) roasting pan

2½ lbs (1.25 kg) beets
Olive oil

1. Peel and trim beets and quarter them vertically. Place beets in roasting pan and drizzle with oil. Toss to coat, then spread out in a single layer. Cover tightly with foil.
2. Roast in preheated oven for 40 to 60 minutes (depending on size of beets), shaking the pan halfway through to prevent sticking, until beets are tender all the way through. Uncover and let cool completely in pan on a wire rack.
3. Transfer to airtight containers and store in the refrigerator for up to 1 week or in the freezer for up to 3 months (thaw overnight in the refrigerator before use).

tip
This recipe will yield about 2 lbs (1 kg) of roasted beets, or about 5 cups (1.25 L) cubed roasted beets.

ROASTED BROCCOLI
(FOR WEEK 5)

Preheat oven to 400°F (200°C)
Rimmed baking sheet

1 lb (500 g) broccoli
Olive oil
Salt

1. Cut broccoli into large florets (about 1 inch/2.5 cm across), including as much stem as you can. Place broccoli on baking

sheet, drizzle with oil and sprinkle with salt. Toss to coat, then spread out in a single layer.

2. Roast, uncovered, in preheated oven for 20 minutes or until edges of florets are browned but broccoli still has a little crispness. Let cool completely on pan on a wire rack.

3. Transfer to airtight containers and store in the refrigerator for up to 1 week.

tip

Your yield from this recipe will be about 4 cups (1 L) roasted broccoli.

ROASTED BROCCOLI AND ONION (FOR WEEK 1)

Preheat oven to 400°F (200°C)
2 rimmed baking sheets

1½ lbs (750 g) broccoli
1 onion, slivered
Olive oil
Salt

1. Cut broccoli into large florets (about 1 inch/2.5 cm across), including as much stem as you can. Divide broccoli and onion between baking sheets, drizzle with oil and sprinkle with salt. Toss to coat, then spread out in a single layer.

2. Roast in preheated oven for 20 minutes or until edges of florets are browned but broccoli still has a little crispness and onions are softened. Let cool completely on pans on wire racks.

3. Transfer to airtight containers and store in the refrigerator for up to 1 week.

tip

Your yield from this recipe will be about 8 cups (2 L) roasted broccoli and onion.

ROASTED BROCCOLINI (FOR WEEK 4)

Preheat oven to 400°F (200°C)
Rimmed baking sheet

1 lb (500 g) broccolini
Olive oil

1. Trim off and discard bases of broccolini stems. Place broccolini on baking sheet and drizzle with oil. Toss to coat, then spread out in a single layer.

2. Roast in preheated oven for 15 minutes or until florets are browned. Let cool completely on pan on a wire rack.

3. Transfer to airtight containers and store in the refrigerator for up to 1 week.

tip

This recipe will yield about 10½ oz (315 g) or 6 cups (1.5 L) roasted broccolini.

ROASTED CARROTS (FOR WEEKS 3 AND 5)

Preheat oven to 400°F (200°C)
2 rimmed baking sheets

Carrots (see tip, page 48)
Olive oil

1. Peel and trim carrots, leaving them whole. Divide carrots between baking sheets, drizzle with oil and roll to coat.

2. Roast in preheated oven for about 30 minutes (depending on width of carrots), shaking the pans and switching their positions halfway through, or until a paring knife inserted into a fat carrot meets no resistance. Let cool completely on pans on wire racks.

3. Slice or chop carrots as desired or leave whole to purée in a soup. Transfer to airtight containers and store in the refrigerator for up to 1 week.

For Week 3, you will need 2½ lbs (1.25 kg) of carrots; for Week 5, you will need 3 lbs (1.5 kg).

Eight ounces (250 g) of raw carrots reduces to about 5 oz (150 g) roasted, or about 1 cup (250 mL) sliced roasted carrots.

ROASTED CAULIFLOWER
(FOR WEEKS 1 AND 2)

Preheat oven to 400°F (200°C)
2 rimmed baking sheets

Cauliflower (see tip)
Olive oil
Salt

1. Cut cauliflower into large florets (about 1 inch/2.5 cm across), including as much stem as you can. Divide cauliflower between baking sheets, drizzle with oil and sprinkle with salt. Toss to coat, then, if you like a nice browned edge, arrange cut side down in a single layer.
2. Roast in preheated oven for 30 minutes, stirring halfway through, until edges of florets are browned and a paring knife pierces thick stems easily. Let cool completely on pans on wire racks.
3. Transfer to airtight containers and store in the refrigerator for up to 1 week.

tips

For Week 1, you will need 2¼ lbs (1.125 kg) of cauliflower; for Week 2, you will need 1 lb 6 oz (600 g).

Seven and a quarter ounces (200 g) of untrimmed raw cauliflower makes about 1 cup (250 mL) roasted florets.

ROASTED WINTER SQUASH
(FOR WEEK 4)

Preheat oven to 400°F (200°C)
Rimmed baking sheet (see tip), lined with parchment paper

7½ lbs (3.75 kg) winter squash (see tips)

1. Halve squash and scoop out seeds with a large spoon. Place squash, cut side down, on prepared baking sheet.
2. Roast in preheated oven for about 40 minutes or until squash is tender when pierced with a paring knife. Turn squash halves over and let cool on pan on a wire rack until cool enough to handle.
3. Place squash, cut side down, on a cutting board and strip off skin. Transfer flesh to airtight containers (don't mash it yet, as you may need some of it left whole to slice). Let cool completely, then store in the refrigerator for up to 1 week. When ready to use, mash, slice or chop squash as directed in your recipe.

tips

You may need 2 baking sheets, depending on the size of the squash and your baking sheets.

Any winter squash, such as butternut, kabocha or red kuri, can be used in this recipe. Very large squash, like Hubbard or full-size pumpkins, will take longer to cook. Smaller squash, like acorn or Sweet Dumpling, will cook more quickly, but have less flesh per pound, so add an extra one to your shopping list.

Each variety of squash will yield a different amount of roasted squash. As a general guideline, a 2½-lb (1.25 kg) butternut squash yields about 1½ lbs (750 g) roasted squash, or about 3 cups (750 mL) mashed roasted squash.

BARLEY

THERE ARE THREE types of barley. The most whole form is called hulled, whole or naked barley, and it has a sturdy bran layer that stays slightly crunchy when cooked. The least whole form, called pearl barley, has had the bran layer scraped off. Pearl barley is the kind you see in soups. Pot barley has had some, but not all, of the bran layer removed. Barley is rich in beta-glucan fiber, which lowers cholesterol, so even pearl barley is considered a nutritious grain because the starches are in the core of the grain.

MAKES 9 TO 10½ CUPS (2.25 TO 2.625 L)

Pinch salt

3 cups (750 mL) hulled, pot or pearl barley

1. Bring a 4-quart (4 L) stockpot of water to a boil and add salt. Add barley and return to a boil. Reduce heat and simmer until tender to the bite, 30 to 40 minutes for pearl barley, 45 to 55 minutes for pot barley or 1 hour for hulled barley. Drain barley.

2. Transfer barley to airtight containers, let cool completely and store in the refrigerator for up to 1 week. Or spread barley out on a baking sheet, place in the freezer until frozen, then transfer to airtight containers and freeze for up to 4 months.

tips

One cup (250 mL) barley makes 3 to 3½ cups (750 to 875 mL) cooked, depending on which type of barley you use.

This recipe makes enough barley for all the recipes in Week 3, plus a little extra.

To reheat (thawed) cooked barley, add it to a saucepan and sprinkle with 1 tbsp (15 mL) water. Cook over medium heat, stirring gently, until hot, adding a few drops of water if it starts to stick. Or place it in a microwave-safe container, sprinkle with 1 to 2 tbsp (15 to 30 mL) water, cover loosely and microwave on High in 1-minute increments, stirring in between, until hot.

BIG-BATCH GRAINS

For the five weeks of this plan, you'll be cooking large batches of grains to use throughout the week: quinoa (page 51) for Weeks 1 and 3, black rice (page 52) for Week 2, barley for Week 3, farro (page 50) for Week 4 and medium-grain brown rice (page 53) for Week 5. Once you have your tubs of cooked grains ready to go, you are set up for breakfasts, lunches and dinners that are full of flavor and nutrition.

FARRO

FARRO IS AVAILABLE in whole and pearled versions. Pearling is the process in which the bran layer is scraped off, leaving the starchy interior. Because farro is Italian, you will see it labeled as perlato (meaning "pearled") or semi-perlato, which has been lightly scraped, leaving some of the bran layer intact. Whole farro is the most nutritious, with the full bran layer intact, and also takes an hour to cook (though it will cook a little faster if you soak it overnight first). Semi-perlato or perlato farro may cook in as little as 20 minutes; check the package instructions and test the grain for doneness.

MAKES ABOUT 12 CUPS (3 L)

Pinch salt

6 cups (1.5 L) whole, perlato or semi-perlato farro

1. Bring a 4-quart (4 L) stockpot of water to a boil and add salt. Add farro and return to a boil. Reduce heat and simmer until tender to the bite, about 20 minutes for perlato or semi-perlato, or 1 hour for whole farro. Drain farro.
2. Transfer farro to airtight containers, let cool completely and store in the refrigerator for up to 1 week. Or spread farro out on a baking sheet, place in the freezer until frozen, then transfer to airtight containers and freeze for up to 4 months.

tips

Semi-perlato and perlato farro can also be cooked the same way as brown rice (see page 53).

One cup (250 mL) farro makes about 2 cups (500 mL) cooked.

This recipe makes enough farro for all the recipes in Week 4, plus a little extra.

To reheat (thawed) cooked farro, add it to a saucepan and sprinkle with 1 tbsp (15 mL) water. Cook over medium heat, stirring gently, until hot, adding a few drops of water if it starts to stick. Or place it in a microwave-safe container, sprinkle with 1 to 2 tbsp (15 to 30 mL) water, cover loosely and microwave on High in 1-minute increments, stirring in between, until hot.

variation

WHEAT BERRIES: If you cannot find farro, you can substitute wheat berries, cooking them as for whole farro.

QUINOA

QUINOA COOKS IN about 15 minutes, making it just as quick as white rice and much more nutritious. It is famous for having more protein than the average grain, but it also provides calcium and lots of minerals.

MAKES ABOUT 18 CUPS (4.5 L)

9¾ cups (2.4 L) water

Pinch salt (optional)

6½ cups (1.6 L) quinoa (see tips)

1. In a 6-quart (6 L) stockpot, bring water to a boil and add salt (if using). Add quinoa and stir once, then return to a boil. Cover tightly, reduce heat to low and simmer for 15 minutes or until quinoa has thrown off its white "halos" and is tender to the bite. Drain off any excess water.
2. Transfer quinoa to airtight containers, let cool completely and store in the refrigerator for up to 1 week. Or spread quinoa out on a baking sheet, place in the freezer until frozen, then transfer to airtight containers and freeze for up to 4 months.

tips

For 6½ cups (1.6 L) quinoa, you'll need to purchase about 2½ lbs (1.25 kg).

This recipe makes enough quinoa for all the recipes in Week 1, plus a little extra; for Week 3, you only need to cook 1¼ cups (300 mL) quinoa in 2 cups (500 mL) water.

For other amounts of quinoa, use 1½ cups (375 mL) water for every 1 cup (250 mL) quinoa. Each cup (250 mL) of raw quinoa will yield about 2½ cups (625 mL) cooked.

To reheat (thawed) cooked quinoa, add it to a saucepan and sprinkle with 1 tbsp (15 mL) water. Cook over medium heat, stirring gently, until hot, adding a few drops of water if it starts to stick. Or place it in a microwave-safe container, sprinkle with 1 to 2 tbsp (15 to 30 mL) water, cover loosely and microwave on High in 1-minute increments, stirring in between, until hot.

BLACK RICE

BLACK RICE IS a medium-grain rice with several different varieties, including one sold under the brand name Forbidden Rice. Although it is also known as purple rice because it often turns purple when cooked, don't confuse it with purple sticky rice, which is sweeter and softer. The different varieties of black rice all have slightly different cooking times and absorb slightly different amounts of water, so check your package and always check for doneness at 25 minutes.

MAKES ABOUT 7½ CUPS (1.875 L)

4½ cups (1.125 L) water

Pinch salt (optional)

3 cups (750 mL) black rice, rinsed and drained

1. In a large pot, bring water to a boil and add salt (if using). Add rice and stir once, then return to a boil. Cover tightly, reduce heat to low and simmer for 25 minutes or until tender. Drain off any excess water.

2. Transfer rice to airtight containers, let cool completely and store in the refrigerator for up to 4 days. Or spread rice out on a baking sheet, place in the freezer until frozen, then transfer to airtight containers and freeze for up to 4 months.

tips

This recipe makes enough rice for all the recipes in Week 2.

For other amounts of black rice, use 1½ cups (375 mL) water for every 1 cup (250 mL) rice. Each cup (250 mL) of raw rice will yield about 2½ cups (625 mL) cooked.

To reheat (thawed) cooked rice, add it to a saucepan and sprinkle with 1 tbsp (15 mL) water. Cook over medium heat, stirring gently, until hot, adding a few drops of water if it starts to stick. Or place it in a microwave-safe container, sprinkle with 1 to 2 tbsp (15 to 30 mL) water, cover loosely and microwave on High in 1-minute increments, stirring in between, until hot.

MEDIUM-GRAIN BROWN RICE

MEDIUM-GRAIN BROWN RICE differs from long-grain in the balance of starches, which makes it a little softer and stickier. It's a wonderfully nutty, satisfyingly filling grain, and it goes with just about everything.

MAKES ABOUT 17 CUPS (4.25 L)

11⅓ cups (2.825 L) water

Pinch salt (optional)

5⅔ cups (1.4 L) medium-grain brown rice, rinsed and drained

1. In a 6-quart (6 L) stockpot, bring water to a boil and add salt (if using). Add rice to the boiling water and stir once, then return to a boil. Cover tightly, reduce heat to low and simmer for 40 to 45 minutes or until tender. Drain off any excess water.
2. Transfer rice to airtight containers, let cool completely and store in the refrigerator for up to 4 days. Or spread rice out on a baking sheet, place in the freezer until frozen, then transfer to airtight containers and freeze for up to 4 months.

tips

This recipe makes enough rice for all the recipes in Week 5.

For other amounts of medium-grain brown rice, use 2 cups (500 mL) boiling water for every 1 cup (250 mL) rice. Each cup (250 mL) of raw rice will yield about 3 cups (750 mL) cooked.

To reheat (thawed) cooked rice, add it to a saucepan and sprinkle with 1 tbsp (15 mL) water. Cook over medium heat, stirring gently, until hot, adding a few drops of water if it starts to stick. Or place it in a microwave-safe container, sprinkle with 1 to 2 tbsp (15 to 30 mL) water, cover loosely and microwave on High in 1-minute increments, stirring in between, until hot.

BLACK BEANS

GETTING INTO THE habit of soaking and cooking dried beans will save you money, and you'll have plenty of protein-rich beans to add to your meals.

MAKES ABOUT 8 CUPS (2 L)

$3\frac{1}{2}$ cups (875 mL) dried black beans (about $1\frac{3}{4}$ lbs/875 g)

Cool water

1. Place beans in a large pot and add 14 cups (3.5 L) cool water. Cover and let soak for at least 4 hours or overnight. Drain, rinse and drain well.
2. Return beans to the pot and add enough cool water to cover by 2 inches (5 cm). Bring to a boil over high heat. Cover, leaving lid slightly ajar, and reduce heat to simmer vigorously but not boil over. Simmer for 45 to 60 minutes or until tender. Drain beans and let cool completely.
3. Transfer beans to airtight containers and store in the refrigerator for up to 1 week. Or spread beans out on a baking sheet, place in the freezer until frozen, then transfer to airtight containers and freeze for up to 4 months.

tips

One cup (250 mL) of dried beans yields about $2\frac{1}{4}$ cups (550 mL) cooked.

This recipe makes enough beans for all of the recipes in Week 4, plus a little extra.

Beans can also be cooked in a pressure cooker for 15 to 20 minutes.

BEAN TIPS

- If buying dried beans in bulk, choose a store that has good turnover. Ask how often they refill the bins; it should be more than once a week. Check dates on packaged dried beans. Beans that are more than a year old take longer to cook and may never get fully tender.
- Soak beans in 4 cups (1 L) cool water per cup (250 mL) of beans, then pour off water and rinse.
- Beans shed some of their hard-to-digest enzymes into the soaking water, so cooking them in fresh water makes them easier to digest.
- If you don't have time to soak, that's okay; just put the beans in a large pot with plenty of water and simmer on low heat for a few hours. It will take longer, but the beans will get done. Just keep the heat low, so they barely bubble, to prevent them from splitting.
- For digestibility, add a piece of kombu seaweed to the pot when you cook the beans. The amino acids in the seaweed help break down the complex starches that create gas in the digestive tract. As a bonus, the kombu also adds minerals to the beans and cooking water.
- You can add salt or seasonings to the pot as the beans cook, contrary to the old adage that salt keeps beans from getting tender. Do not add anything acidic, like citrus juice, wine or vinegar.
- To test a bean, scoop one out and let it cool for a couple of minutes before biting it; hot beans will seem softer than cool ones.

CHICKPEAS AND AQUAFABA

DON'T THROW AWAY that chickpea water! Low, slow cooking enriches the cooking water, making it good for use as aquafaba. If you have time, the long method will make a thicker, more fully extracted aquafaba, but the short method works too.

MAKES ABOUT 7½ CUPS (1.875 L) CHICKPEAS AND 2½ CUPS (625 ML) AQUAFABA

2½ cups (625 mL) dried chickpeas (about 1 lb/500 g)

Water

1 strip kombu (optional)

SOAKING

1. Place chickpeas in a large pot and add enough cool water to cover by 3 inches (7.5 cm). Cover and let soak for at least 6 hours or overnight. Drain, rinse and drain well.

COOKING: LONG METHOD

2. Return chickpeas to the pot and add 7 cups (1.75 L) cool water and kombu (if using). Bring to a boil over high heat. Reduce heat to low and simmer for about 4 hours or until chickpeas are tender but not falling apart. (Alternatively, cook chickpeas in a slow cooker on Low for about 8 hours.)

3. If time permits, let chickpeas cool completely in the cooking water and chill overnight, to let the water become thick and gelatinous.

4. Place a strainer over a large bowl and drain chickpeas. Transfer aquafaba and chickpeas to separate storage containers and store in the refrigerator for up to 1 week.

COOKING: SHORT METHOD

2. Transfer chickpeas to the pot and add enough cool water to cover by 2 inches (5 cm). Bring to a boil over high heat. Cover, leaving lid slightly ajar, and reduce heat to simmer strongly but not boil over. Simmer for 1½ to 2 hours or until tender. (Alternatively, cook chickpeas in a pressure cooker for 10 minutes.)

3. Place a strainer over a large bowl and drain chickpeas. Transfer aquafaba and chickpeas to separate storage containers and store in the refrigerator for up to 1 week. When you have time, boil aquafaba to reduce it to 2½ cups (625 mL).

tips

One cup (250 mL) dried chickpeas yields about 3 cups (750 mL) cooked.

This recipe makes enough for Week 1, plus a little extra. For Week 2, you'll only need to cook 1 cup (250 mL) chickpeas.

To freeze chickpeas, spread them out on a baking sheet, place in the freezer until frozen, then transfer to airtight containers and freeze for up to 4 months.

Freeze aquafaba in small airtight containers for up to 4 months. Thaw in the refrigerator overnight.

BAKED MARINATED TOFU

THIS TOFU IS a versatile prep item, ready to go into sandwiches, stir-fries and other dishes with no frying or extra prep time. The baking time is flexible, depending on both the tofu and your taste (see tip).

MAKES 20 SLICES

Large square food storage tub (preferably 10 inches/25 cm square)

2 large rimmed baking sheets, lined with parchment paper

24 oz (750 g) water-packed extra-firm tofu

2 tbsp (30 mL) packed light brown sugar

½ tsp (2 mL) cayenne pepper

½ cup (125 mL) tamari

½ cup (125 mL) unsweetened apple juice

2 tbsp (30 mL) toasted (dark) sesame oil

1. Drain tofu and wrap in clean tea towels, pressing gently to remove excess water. Cut each block of tofu into ten ½-inch (1 cm) slices and place in storage tub.
2. In a small bowl, whisk together brown sugar, cayenne, tamari, apple juice and sesame oil. Pour over tofu. Seal the lid and shake container gently to coat all the slices. Flip container carefully to move marinade between the slices. Refrigerate overnight.
3. Preheat oven to 400°F (200°C).
4. Remove tofu slices from marinade and place on prepared baking sheets, spacing them apart. Drizzle tops with a little marinade. Discard the remaining marinade.
5. Bake for 40 minutes (see tip), turning tofu slices with a spatula and reversing the positions of the pans halfway through. Let cool completely on pans on wire racks.
6. Transfer cooled tofu to airtight containers and store in the refrigerator for up to 1 week or in the freezer for up to 4 months.

tips

Water-packed tofu comes in varying levels of firmness, from soft to extra-firm. The firmer it is, the more water has been pressed out before it was packaged. Aseptic-packaged tofu is silken tofu, which is too soft for this method.

Extra-firm tofu, made with a little extra nigari coagulant and pressed longer, is already so dense that it will be chewy and firm within 40 minutes of baking. If you use standard firm tofu instead, it will be coated and have crispy edges in 40 minutes, but to get a nice, dense texture, give it a full hour.

For a more flavor-infused, chewier tofu, slice the tofu as in step 1 and freeze it until solid, then thaw in the refrigerator and proceed with step 2.

BAKED MARINATED TEMPEH

IF YOU LIKE lots of texture, tempeh is for you. A chunky, fermented block of tempeh is a slightly mushroomy, umami-rich protein that will save your week when it's baked with a tasty marinade. The combo of tamari, maple and smoky paprika is irresistible.

MAKES ABOUT 96 SLICES

Steamer basket

6-cup (1.5 L) square or rectangular food storage tub

2 large rimmed baking sheets, lined with parchment paper

2 lbs (1 kg) tempeh

1 cup (250 mL) unsweetened apple juice

½ cup (125 mL) tamari

¼ cup (60 mL) extra virgin olive oil

¼ cup (60 mL) pure maple syrup

2 tbsp (30 mL) unseasoned rice vinegar

1 tsp (5 mL) smoked paprika

1. Add tempeh to a steamer basket set over a pot of boiling water, stacking as needed, cover and steam for 5 minutes. Transfer tempeh to a cutting board to cool. When cool enough to handle, cut into ⅓-inch (0.75 cm) slices.

2. In storage tub, whisk together apple juice, tamari, oil, maple syrup, vinegar and paprika. Place tempeh in marinade, arranging slices to fit loosely in the container. Seal the lid and flip container a few times, coating tempeh with marinade. Refrigerate overnight.

3. Preheat oven to 400°F (200°C).

4. Remove tempeh slices from marinade and place on prepared baking sheets, spacing them apart. Drizzle the remaining marinade over top.

5. Bake for 15 minutes. Use a spatula to turn tempeh slices over. Reverse the position of the pans on the racks and bake for 10 minutes. Let cool completely on pans on wire racks.

6. Transfer cooled tempeh to airtight containers and store in the refrigerator for up to 1 week or in the freezer for up to 3 months.

tips

There are many kinds of tempeh. Some are made with added grains, such as wild rice, or even veggies. Experiment with any that sounds good to you.

SMOKY TEMPEH TACO MEAT

TACOS ARE A favorite food for many of us, so this "meat" will come in handy for quick meals. It's also great in burritos, over salad or simply scooped up with chips.

MAKES 8 SERVINGS (ABOUT 4 CUPS/1 L)

2 tbsp (30 mL) extra virgin olive oil

2 onions, chopped

4 cloves garlic, chopped

1 lb (500 g) tempeh, chopped (see tip)

4 tsp (20 mL) chili powder

2 tsp (10 mL) smoked paprika

2 tsp (10 mL) dried oregano

1½ tsp (7 mL) salt

1 cup (250 mL) ready-to-use reduced-sodium vegetable broth or Homemade Veggie Stock (page 59)

1. In a large skillet, heat oil over medium-high heat. Add onions and cook, stirring, until starting to sizzle. Reduce heat to medium and cook, stirring, for about 5 minutes or until softened.
2. Add garlic and tempeh; cook, stirring, for 3 to 4 minutes or until tempeh is browned and starting to stick. Sprinkle with chili powder, paprika, oregano and salt; stir, then stir in broth. Cook, stirring, until pan is nearly dry.
3. Transfer tempeh to an airtight container, let cool completely and store in the refrigerator for up to 1 week or in the freezer for up to 4 months.

tip

Chop the tempeh to make a texture similar to ground beef. If you have a food processor, you can use the steel blade to pulse cubed tempeh into a chunky mince.

variation

If you like spicier tacos, substitute 1 tsp (5 mL) chipotle chile powder (or to taste) for the smoked paprika.

HOMEMADE VEGGIE STOCK

VEGETABLE STOCK IS a valuable asset in the vegan kitchen, adding extra flavor and nutrients to soups, sauces and cooked grains. This stock is made as quickly as possible with the help of your blender. Finely chopping the vegetables in the water, then simmering them gently for half an hour allows you to extract their essence in a flash. This recipe makes a gallon of stock, but you can easily halve or even quarter it to save space.

MAKES ABOUT 16 CUPS (4 L)

Blender

2-cup or 1-quart (500 mL or 1 L) mason jars

16 cups (4 L) water, divided

8 large carrots, cut into 2-inch (5 cm) chunks

4 cloves garlic, peeled

2 large onions, peeled and quartered

1 small bunch celery (about 12 stalks), cut into 2-inch (5 cm) chunks

2 cups (500 mL) parsley stems

12 sprigs fresh thyme

4 large bay leaves

4 tsp (20 mL) black peppercorns

2 tsp (10 mL) salt (approx.)

Freshly ground black pepper (optional)

1. Pour 4 cups (1 L) water in the blender. Add one-quarter of the carrots, garlic, onions, celery and parsley stems. Pulse four or five times, just until vegetables are finely chopped. Pour water and vegetables into a 6-quart (6 L) stockpot. Repeat until all the vegetables are chopped.

2. Stir vegetables and place over high heat. Add thyme, bay leaves, peppercorns and salt. Bring to a boil, stirring. Reduce heat and simmer gently for 30 minutes.

3. Strain stock into a heatproof container, using the back of a spoon to press lightly on the vegetables, pressing out more liquid.

4. Taste stock. If you want a more concentrated flavor, return it to the pot and bring to a boil over high heat, then reduce heat and simmer vigorously until reduced as desired. Taste and adjust seasoning with salt and pepper as desired.

5. Let cool completely, then transfer to jars, cover tightly and refrigerate for up to 1 week or freeze for up to 4 months.

tips

Use up those slightly over-the-hill vegetables for this, but trim off any brown spots and remove anything slimy.

Don't boil the stock, or it will be bitter.

variation

For an Asian stock, add a hunk of fresh gingerroot and skip the thyme. Season the finished stock with soy sauce.

QUICK MISO SOUP

TRADITIONAL MISO SOUP uses dashi, a stock made from seaweed and dried fish. This vegan version uses vegetable broth for a fish-free flavorful base. You'll be using roasted carrots when you make it to accompany the sushi bowls in Week 5, but in the future, you can use any vegetable you have lying about. Miso is famous for containing active probiotics and enzymes, which is why you simply stir it in and don't let it boil, so you get the full benefits.

MAKES 4 SERVINGS (ABOUT 5 CUPS/1.25 L)

4 cups (1 L) ready-to-use reduced-sodium vegetable broth or Homemade Veggie Stock (page 59)

4 green onions, thinly sliced

2 cups (500 mL) chopped roasted carrots (see page 47)

1 tsp (5 mL) grated gingerroot

1/4 cup (60 mL) white miso

1/2 tsp (2 mL) unseasoned rice vinegar

1/4 cup (60 mL) water

1. Pour broth into a large pot and place over high heat. Add green onions, carrots and ginger; bring to a vigorous boil. Reduce heat and simmer until carrots are warmed through.
2. Meanwhile, place miso and vinegar in a cup and stir in water, mashing miso to make a smooth paste.
3. Turn off heat and stir miso mixture into pot. Serve immediately or let cool completely.
4. To store, transfer cooled soup to airtight containers and store in the refrigerator for up to 4 days. Reheat gently, just until hot, to preserve the miso.

tips

Misos range from mild white and yellow to darker brown. Darker miso is stronger-tasting, so if you substitute it, you'll want to use a little less.

Serve topped with 1 sheet of crumbled nori, divided among the bowls, if desired. If storing the soup before serving, wait to add the nori until right before serving.

This recipe is very scalable, so go ahead and double it if you want to serve more people.

variation

Try this recipe with ready-to-use mushroom broth in place of the vegetable broth and sautéed mushrooms in place of the carrots, for a deeply flavorful mushroom miso soup.

VEGGIE SPAGHETTI SAUCE

SPAGHETTI SAUCE IS the perfect vehicle for veggies and herbs, and when you make your own, you know it's all good. Once you have this sauce in the fridge, you are set for some great meals.

MAKES ABOUT 4 CUPS (1 L)

1 tbsp (15 mL) extra virgin olive oil

1 onion, chopped

½ cup (125 mL) diced carrot

2 cloves garlic, minced

1 tbsp (15 mL) fresh thyme, chopped

14-oz (398 mL) can tomato purée

14-oz (398 mL) can diced tomatoes, with juice

¼ cup (60 mL) red wine

2 tbsp (30 mL) tomato paste

½ tsp (2 mL) dried basil

½ tsp (2 mL) dried oregano

½ cup (125 mL) chopped fresh parsley

Salt and freshly ground black pepper

1. In a medium pot, heat oil over medium-high heat. Add onion and carrot; cook, stirring, until starting to sizzle. Reduce heat to medium-low and cook, stirring occasionally, for at least 10 minutes or until very soft. Add garlic and thyme; cook, stirring, for about 4 minutes or until onions are light golden.

2. Stir in tomato purée, diced tomatoes, wine, tomato paste, basil and oregano; bring to a simmer. Reduce heat and simmer, stirring every 10 minutes or so, for 20 to 30 minutes or until thick. Stir in parsley and cook for 2 minutes. Season to taste with salt and pepper. Serve immediately or let cool completely.

3. To store, transfer cooled sauce to airtight containers and store in the refrigerator for up to 1 week or in the freezer for 4 months. Thaw overnight in the refrigerator, if frozen, then reheat in the microwave or in a saucepan over medium heat, stirring often, until heated through.

tips

Use ½ cup (125 mL) sauce per serving of pasta.

When fresh basil is in season, substitute a handful of fresh for the dried basil.

If you have room in your freezer, go ahead and make a double batch of this sauce.

CREAMY CHEESY SAUCE

THIS CASHEW-BASED SAUCE really does the job, answering your cheesy cravings with plant-based goodness. Equally good in mac and cheese, nachos and wraps, it's sure to become a staple in your household.

MAKES ABOUT 2½ CUPS (625 ML)

Blender

1 cup (250 mL) raw cashews

Cold water

2 cloves garlic, sliced

¼ cup (60 mL) arrowroot starch

¼ cup (60 mL) nutritional yeast

1 tsp (5 mL) salt

¼ tsp (1 mL) ground turmeric

1½ cups (375 mL) unsweetened plain soy milk

¼ cup (60 mL) canola oil

2 tbsp (30 mL) red miso

1 tsp (5 mL) freshly squeezed lemon juice

1. Place cashews in a bowl and add enough cold water to cover. Soak at room temperature for at least 6 hours (see tip). Drain well.
2. In blender, combine cashews, garlic, arrowroot, yeast, salt, turmeric, soy milk, oil, miso and lemon juice; blend until smooth.
3. Transfer cashew mixture to a small saucepan over medium heat. Bring to a boil, whisking constantly, and boil, whisking, for about 5 minutes or until thickened, reducing the heat if the sauce starts to stick. Serve immediately or let cool completely.
4. To store, transfer cooled sauce to an airtight container and store in the refrigerator for up to 1 week. Reheat in the microwave or in a saucepan over medium heat, stirring, until heated through.

tips

Place your soaking cashews in the refrigerator; if you don't get around to making this sauce right away, they will keep for a week.

If you like spice, add a pinch of cayenne pepper in step 2, just to warm the sauce up without making it really spicy.

If your cheesy cravings are strong, you can make a double batch of this sauce.

variation

NACHO SAUCE: Measure ½ cup (125 mL) sauce per serving. Into each, stir in 4 chopped cherry tomatoes and ¼ tsp (1 mL) chipotle chile powder. Reheat, if needed, and serve over chips or as a dip.

CREAMY CAULIFLOWER SAUCE

CAULIFLOWER HAS BECOME the go-to veggie, in part because it's a chameleon. In this recipe, mild white cauliflower disappears into a creamy sauce, giving you a lighter version of the Creamy Cheesy Sauce (page 62). It's not as rich as that one either, so let that inform your choice of which one to make.

MAKES ABOUT 2¼ CUPS (550 ML)

Blender

2 tbsp (30 mL) melted coconut oil

1 onion, chopped

2 cloves garlic, chopped

3 cups (750 mL) chopped cauliflower (about ½ large head)

1 carrot, chopped

½ cup (125 mL) dry white wine

¼ cup (60 mL) unsweetened plain soy milk

6 tbsp (90 mL) nutritional yeast

1 tsp (5 mL) salt

1. In a large skillet, heat coconut oil over medium heat. Add onion and cook, stirring, for about 5 minutes or until softened. Add garlic and cook, stirring, for 1 minute.
2. Stir in cauliflower and carrot. Add wine, cover and steam for 10 minutes. Uncover and cook, stirring occasionally, until pan is almost dry. Remove from heat.
3. Pour milk into blender, then add cauliflower mixture, yeast and salt. Purée until very smooth, scraping down the sides of the container as needed.
4. If serving immediately, transfer sauce to a medium saucepan and warm over medium heat, if desired.
5. To store, transfer sauce to an airtight container, let cool completely and store in the refrigerator for up to 4 days or in the freezer for up to 4 months. Thaw overnight in the refrigerator, if frozen, then reheat in the microwave or in a saucepan over medium heat, stirring often, until heated through.

tips

This plant-based purée is lighter than the Creamy Cheesy Sauce, and you can use it in the same way if you are cutting back on calories.

If you have a big head of cauliflower, go ahead and make a double batch of this sauce.

variation

NACHO SAUCE: Spice up the sauce by adding a chopped tomato and hot pepper sauce to taste. Reheat, if needed, and serve over chips or as a dip.

MANGO SRIRACHA SAUCE

IF YOU WANT a taste of the tropics without leaving home, make this sauce. The creamy mango purée is spiked with just enough heat to make it interesting. Use it as an all-purpose hot sauce or as a fantastic dip for chips or veggies.

MAKES ABOUT 1 CUP (250 ML)

Blender

1 large mango, coarsely chopped

1 slice fresh turmeric

½ tsp (2 mL) salt

2 tbsp (30 mL) pure maple syrup

1 tbsp (15 mL) freshly squeezed lemon juice

2 tsp (10 mL) Sriracha

1. In blender, combine mango, turmeric, salt, maple syrup, lemon juice and Sriracha; purée until very smooth, scraping down the sides of the container as needed.
2. Transfer to a bowl and serve, or transfer to an airtight container and store in the refrigerator for up to 4 days.

tip

Select a ripe mango that yields to a gentle squeeze. If all the mangos in the store are hard and green, let yours ripen in a sunny window for a few days to develop its flavor.

variation

For a slightly different spin, use lime juice instead of lemon juice or try a different hot sauce in place of the Sriracha.

TOMATO CILANTRO SALSA

A TASTY FRESH salsa can make a meal, whether you use it with burritos or tacos or as a dip for chips. This one comes together with just a few strokes of the knife, delivering fresh flavors to everything you pair it with.

MAKES ABOUT 2 CUPS (500 ML)

1 large jalapeño pepper, seeded and chopped

1 clove garlic, minced

½ green bell pepper, chopped

10 oz (300 g) tomatoes (about 2 large), chopped

¼ cup (60 mL) packed fresh cilantro, chopped

1 tsp (5 mL) ground cumin

1 tsp (5 mL) salt

½ tsp (2 mL) freshly ground black pepper

1 tbsp (15 mL) freshly squeezed lime juice

1. In a medium bowl, combine jalapeño, garlic, green pepper, tomatoes, cilantro, cumin, salt, pepper and lime juice.
2. Serve immediately or cover tightly and store in the refrigerator for up to 2 days.

tips

This is a medium salsa. For a little more heat, you can add more jalapeño or substitute hotter chiles, like serranos.

Pack a cup of salsa to take for lunch with any Mexican-style meal.

BASIL PESTO

BASIL PESTO MIGHT be the purest expression of the glory of basil. But pesto is more than just a classic pasta sauce — a jar of it is a versatile timesaver, making vegetables irresistible and elevating pizza, crostini and bagels.

MAKES ABOUT 1½ CUPS (375 ML)

Mini chopper or immersion blender

3 cloves garlic, chopped

3 cups (750 mL) packed fresh basil leaves

1½ cups (375 mL) packed spinach leaves

¾ cup (175 mL) pine nuts, toasted (see tip)

¾ tsp (3 mL) salt

¾ cup (175 mL) extra virgin olive oil

1. In the mini chopper or using an immersion blender in a tall cup, purée garlic, basil, spinach, pine nuts, salt and oil until very smooth, scraping down the sides of the container as needed.
2. Transfer to a bowl and serve, or transfer to an airtight container and store in the refrigerator for up to 4 days.

tips

Chlorophyll-rich spinach helps keep the pesto from turning brown when it is stored.

Toast pine nuts in a small skillet over medium heat, stirring and shaking constantly, for about 3 minutes or until light golden. Transfer to a bowl to cool.

If you have a food processor or a high-speed blender, these appliances will also work well for this recipe. If using the blender, add the oil first, then the other ingredients.

variations

Substitute arugula for the basil.

Use half basil and half parsley.

If you don't have pine nuts, try walnuts or almonds.

SUPER-CREAMY HUMMUS

IF YOU LEARN only one trick from this book, this one is worth the price of admission. A gentle rub in a bowl of cold water loosens the skins from chickpeas so you can scoop them up and discard them. The resulting purée is so much smoother than hummus made with skins, you will never go back to the old way. And once you become addicted, you'll be glad there are so many variations!

MAKES ABOUT 2½ CUPS (625 ML)

Mini chopper or immersion blender

2 cups (500 mL) cooked chickpeas (see page 55)

Cold water

2 cloves garlic, chopped

½ tsp (2 mL) salt (or to taste)

¾ cup (175 mL) tahini

½ cup (125 mL) ice water (approx.)

3 tbsp (45 mL) freshly squeezed lemon juice

Extra virgin olive oil

Paprika

1. Place chickpeas in a large bowl and cover with plenty of cold water. Squeeze and knead beans underwater to slip off skins. Scoop up and discard skins as they float to the surface. Drain chickpeas.

2. In the mini chopper or using an immersion blender in a tall cup, purée chickpeas, garlic, salt, tahini, ice water and lemon juice until smooth, scraping down the sides of the container as needed. If the mixture is too thick, add more ice water, 1 tsp (5 mL) at a time.

3. To serve immediately, spread in a bowl, drizzle with olive oil and sprinkle with paprika. To store, transfer to an airtight container and store in the refrigerator for up to 1 week. Wait to add the oil and paprika until just before serving.

tips

If your mini chopper holds less than 3 cups (750 mL), you will need to prepare this recipe in batches.

If you have a food processor or a high-speed blender, these appliances will also work well for this recipe. If using the blender, add the ice water and lemon juice first, then the other ingredients.

add-ins (pick one)

Add your choice of add-in (pick one from the list below) with the chickpeas in step 2, saving some of the add-in to garnish the dip in the serving bowl. Add about 2 tbsp (30 mL) more lemon juice (to taste). Taste and adjust the salt as needed.

- 1 jar (8 oz/250 mL) roasted red pepper, drained and patted dry
- 1 large avocado
- ½ cup (125 mL) sun-dried tomatoes, rehydrated and minced
- 6 canned or marinated artichoke hearts, drained
- 1 bulb roasted garlic
- 2 small chipotle chile peppers, in adobo sauce
- ¼ cup (60 mL) pesto

AQUAFABA MAYO

GIVING UP EGGS needn't mean giving up mayo. "Aquafaba" is the term for the water (aqua) left over from cooking beans (faba), and it's a brilliant egg replacer. A base of creamy cashews and aquafaba, with lemon juice and plenty of olive oil, makes a pretty fair approximation of the mayo spread you grew up eating on your sandwiches. It's also good for potato salads and other dishes that call for mayonnaise.

MAKES ABOUT 1 CUP (250 ML)

Blender

¼ cup (60 mL) raw cashews

Cold water

½ tsp (2 mL) salt

¼ tsp (1 mL) garlic powder

¼ cup (60 mL) aquafaba (see tips)

1 tbsp (15 mL) freshly squeezed lemon juice

2 tsp (10 mL) Dijon mustard

¼ cup (60 mL) canola oil

¼ cup (60 mL) extra virgin olive oil

1. Place cashews in a bowl and add enough cold water to cover. Soak for at least 6 hours or overnight. Drain well.
2. In blender, combine cashews, salt, garlic powder, aquafaba, lemon juice and mustard; blend, starting on a low speed and increasing until cashews are smoothly puréed, scraping down the sides of the container as needed.
3. Remove plug from lid and replace lid. Start on low speed, increase to high speed and blend for 4 minutes. At that point, start very slowly drizzling in canola oil in a thin stream. It should take a couple of minutes to incorporate it. Drizzle in olive oil the same way.
4. Scrape mayo into an airtight container and refrigerate for up to 1 week. It will thicken more as it chills.

tips

When you cook chickpeas (see page 55) or use a can of chickpeas, save the aquafaba in ¼-cup (60 mL) portions in the freezer for making this mayo.

If using aquafaba from canned chickpeas, purchase unsalted chickpeas or use half as much salt in the recipe.

variations

GARLIC AÏOLI: Add a clove of crushed garlic at the end of step 3 and pulse to blend.

RED PEPPER AÏOLI: Add ½ roasted red pepper, drained, at the end of step 3 and pulse to blend.

CASHEW PARMESAN

IT'S SO MUCH fun to sprinkle this over your favorite Italian dishes, you might want to add it to everything. Don't hold back — you are adding "nooch" and the B_{12} you need, as well as tasty cheesiness. The cashews give it a little creamy, nutty yum factor too.

MAKES ABOUT 2½ CUPS (625 ML) | Preheat oven to 300°F (150°C)

Baking sheet

Mini chopper or immersion blender

5 oz (150 g) white baguette, crusts removed (or 2 hamburger buns, crusts shaved off)

½ cup (125 mL) raw cashews

¼ cup (60 mL) nutritional yeast

1 tsp (5 mL) salt

½ tsp (2 mL) granulated garlic (optional)

1. Slice baguette (or buns) and spread slices at one end of baking sheet. Spread cashews at the other. Bake in preheated oven for 10 minutes or until nuts are lightly toasted and bread is dry and crisp but not browned (see tip).
2. In mini chopper or using an immersion blender in a tall cup, pulse cashews until finely chopped. Transfer to an airtight container.
3. Tear bread into chunks and, in mini chopper or using immersion blender in a tall cup, in batches as necessary, pulse bread into large crumbs.
4. Add bread crumbs to cashews and stir in yeast, salt and garlic (if using).
5. Use immediately or store in the refrigerator for up to 2 weeks.

tips

If, after 10 minutes in the oven, the bread is still moist enough to sink in when you poke it in the middle, use a spatula to transfer cashews to a bowl and return bread to the oven for 5 minutes or until dry and crisp but not browned.

If you have a food processor or a high-speed blender, these appliances will also work well for steps 2 and 3 of this recipe.

BREAKFASTS

QUINOA TOFU SCRAMBLE

START YOUR MORNING right with a one-two punch of protein from tofu and quinoa, seasoned with some Mexican flair. There's so much texture and flavor in this scramble, it will wake you up and energize you for the day.

MAKES 4 SERVINGS

12 oz (375 g) extra-firm tofu (see tip)

2 green onions, chopped

1 large red bell pepper, chopped

2 cups (500 mL) cooked quinoa (see page 51)

¾ tsp (3 mL) salt

½ tsp (2 mL) chipotle chile powder

½ tsp (2 mL) dried oregano

½ cup (125 mL) green pumpkin seeds (pepitas)

Canola oil (optional)

1. Drain tofu and wrap in a clean kitchen towel, pressing lightly to extract as much water as possible.
2. In a large bowl, crumble tofu with your hands. Add green onions, red pepper, quinoa, salt, chile powder and oregano. Mix well, crumbling tofu further and mashing it all together.
3. In a large nonstick or cast-iron skillet, toast pumpkin seeds over medium-high heat, swirling and shaking seeds until they start to pop and some are lightly browned. Transfer to a plate and let cool.
4. Return skillet to medium-high heat. If using a cast-iron pan, drizzle in a little canola oil. Add tofu mixture and cook, scraping the bottom of the pan every minute or so, until starting to sizzle. Reduce heat to medium and cook, stirring and scraping, for about 5 minutes or until tofu is browned and pepper is softened. Serve sprinkled with pumpkin seeds.

tips

For the best texture, buy water-packed extra-firm tofu for this dish.

Each serving will be about 1¼ cups (300 mL). Leftovers can be cooled and stored in an airtight container in the refrigerator for up to 4 days.

variation

Use sunflower seeds instead of pumpkin seeds for a little variety.

MAPLE GRANOLA
WITH ALMONDS AND RAISINS

IF YOU HAVE a cereal habit, you need to bump the box and make your own granola. Organic oats, real maple syrup and extra virgin olive oil will make a higher-quality cereal than you can buy in a box, and you'll save money too.

MAKES ABOUT 7 CUPS (1.75 L) | Preheat oven to 300°F (150°C)

2 baking sheets, lined with parchment paper

4 cups (1 L) large-flake (old-fashioned) rolled oats

1 cup (250 mL) almonds, coarsely chopped

¼ cup (60 mL) ground flax seeds (flaxseed meal)

½ cup (125 mL) pure maple syrup

½ cup (125 mL) extra virgin olive oil

1 tsp (5 mL) vanilla extract

½ tsp (2 mL) salt

1 cup (250 mL) raisins

Unsweetened plain soy milk

1. In a large bowl, stir together oats, almonds and flax seeds.
2. In a medium bowl, whisk together maple syrup, oil, vanilla and salt. Pour over oat mixture and stir to coat thoroughly. Spread mixture out on baking sheets.
3. Bake in preheated oven, stirring and reversing the positions of the pans in the oven every 15 minutes, for 1 hour or until granola is quite golden and toasted-looking.
4. Sprinkle raisins over hot granola on pans and mix well. Let cool completely on wire racks, then transfer to an airtight container and store at room temperature for up to 2 weeks.
5. To serve, add ½ cup (125 mL) granola to each bowl and pour in ½ cup (125 mL) milk.

tip

Extra virgin olive oils have distinctive flavors, from peppery to fruity. The oil will give this granola a surprisingly delicious olive flavor. Try it with different oils and find your favorite.

variation

If you're into virgin coconut oil for its health benefits, you can use that instead of olive oil, for a hint of coconut.

JARS OF OATS
WITH BERRIES AND COCONUT YOGURT

COOKING OATS IS so old-fashioned — why turn on the stove when you can simply soak? A comfortingly familiar whole grain, rolled oats have the ability to drink up all the liquid needed to soften and flavor them. And instead of plumping them with water, you'll be adding all the nutrition of soy milk and yogurt, making this breakfast even better for you.

MAKES 4 SERVINGS

Four 1-pint (500 mL) mason jars or 2-cup (500 mL) food storage containers

2 cups (500 mL) large-flake (old-fashioned) rolled oats

2 cups (500 mL) vanilla-flavored or plain soy milk

2 cups (500 mL) fresh or frozen berries (see tip)

2 cups (500 mL) coconut milk yogurt

¼ cup (60 mL) chia seeds

½ cup (125 mL) almonds

1. Divide oats and milk evenly among jars, stirring to combine. Top with berries, then yogurt, chia seeds and almonds, dividing evenly.
2. Cover tightly and refrigerate for at least 4 hours, to soak the oats, or for up to 4 days. Stir before serving.

tips

Using frozen berries will save you money when berries are not in season, and the berries will thaw as they sit in the refrigerator overnight, tinting the oats a lovely shade.

These jars are also great as a snack!

variation

Sprinkle with ground flax seeds instead of chia seeds.

SWEET POTATO PIE SKIN-SAVER SMOOTHIES

SWEET POTATO IS a great source of powerful vitamin A, which both prevents skin aging by boosting collagen production and fights acne. Pumpkin pie–flavored drinks and foods are all the rage, and it's far better to enjoy freshly baked sweet potato and real spice.

MAKES 4 SERVINGS

Blender

2 cups (500 mL) plain soy yogurt

1 cup (250 mL) mashed baked sweet potato (see page 45)

½ cup (125 mL) almond butter

2 tbsp (30 mL) pure maple syrup

2 tbsp (30 mL) golden flax seeds

1 tsp (5 mL) pumpkin pie spice

1 tsp (5 mL) vanilla extract

1 cup (250 mL) ice cubes

1. In blender, combine yogurt, sweet potato, almond butter, maple syrup, flax seeds, pumpkin pie spice, vanilla and ice cubes; blend to the desired consistency, scraping down the sides of the container as needed. Serve immediately.

tips

You can use canned pumpkin purée (not pie filling) in place of the sweet potato in this smoothie, but it will not be as sweet.

Ice cubes give the smoothie a lighter texture that is similar to ice cream.

When making smoothies, place the ingredients in the blender in the order given, with the liquid ingredients first. This will allow the blender to work most effectively.

QUINOA AND MANGO BREAKFAST BOWLS

THIS BOWL IS so easy to prepare, and so full of colors, textures and spice, that everyone will be happy, including the cook.

MAKES 4 SERVINGS

4 cups (1 L) cooked quinoa (see page 51)

1 tsp (5 mL) ground cinnamon

1 cup (250 mL) unsweetened plain soy milk

2 Ataulfo mangos, halved and scored (or 2 cups/500 mL cubed mango)

2 cups (500 mL) plain soy yogurt

½ cup (125 mL) pistachios, chopped

Ground cinnamon

1. In a medium pot, combine quinoa, cinnamon and milk. Heat, stirring, over medium heat until hot.
2. Divide quinoa mixture among four bowls and top with mangos, yogurt and pistachios, dividing evenly. Sprinkle with cinnamon.

 tip

To score mangos, use a chef's knife to slice the flesh from the pit, making two flat "cheeks" of fruit. Place the fruit, skin side down, on the cutting board and use a paring knife to score the flesh in squares by cutting down to but not through the skin. Pull back the edges of the skin to open up the mango squares and place each half, skin side down, on top of a prepared bowl.

MICROWAVE METHOD Prepare individual bowls of quinoa, milk and cinnamon; microwave each on High for 2 minutes or until hot. Stir well and top as directed.

CRANBERRY MUESLI
WITH PECANS

BRIGHT RED CRANBERRIES are loaded with potent antioxidants and also tint your oats a lovely pink in this breakfast muesli. Pecans add crunchy bits that enliven your bowl even more.

MAKES 4 SERVINGS

8-cup (2 L) food storage container (microwave-safe if serving warm)

2 cups (500 mL) large-flake (old-fashioned) rolled oats

2 cups (500 mL) unsweetened plain soy milk

1 cup (250 mL) unsweetened cranberry juice

1 cup (250 mL) dried cranberries

2 cups (500 mL) plain soy yogurt

1/4 cup (60 mL) pecan halves, chopped

2 tbsp (30 mL) pure maple syrup

TO SERVE COLD

1. Place oats in the storage container and stir in milk and cranberry juice. Stir in cranberries and yogurt. Cover tightly and refrigerate for at least 4 hours, to soak the oats, or for up to 4 days.
2. Divide oat mixture among four bowls. Top each with 1 tbsp (15 mL) pecans and drizzle with maple syrup.

TO SERVE WARM

1. Place oats in the storage container and stir in milk and cranberry juice. Stir in cranberries. Cover tightly and refrigerate for at least 4 hours, to soak the oats, or for up to 4 days.
2. Divide oat mixture among four bowls and microwave each on High for 2 minutes or until hot.
3. Stir yogurt into each bowl, dividing evenly. Top each with 1 tbsp (15 mL) pecans and drizzle with maple syrup. Serve immediately.

tip

Soy milk and yogurt offer the most protein of all the nondairy options. If you substitute another nondairy milk and yogurt in this recipe, you'll want to consider adding more protein to the meal.

variation

Try this with dried blueberries in place of cranberries for variety.

LEMON PECAN MUFFINS
WITH APRICOT CASHEW SPREAD

THESE LOVABLE MUFFINS have the crunch of pecans and the fragrant tang of lemon zest to make them a cut above. That they are whole grain and vegan can stay our little secret. Serve 2 muffins per serving for breakfast and save the rest for snacks or dessert later in the week.

MAKES 12 MUFFINS | Preheat oven to 375°F (190°C)

12-cup muffin pan, lined with paper liners

2 cups (500 mL) white whole wheat flour or whole wheat pastry flour

1 cup + 3 tbsp (250 mL + 45 mL) large-flake (old-fashioned) rolled oats, divided

1 cup (250 mL) granulated sugar

1 tbsp (15 mL) grated lemon zest

1 tsp (5 mL) baking powder

½ tsp (2 mL) baking soda

½ tsp (2 mL) salt

¾ cup (175 mL) unsweetened plain soy milk

2 tbsp (30 mL) ground chia seeds

2 tbsp (30 mL) freshly squeezed lemon juice

½ cup (125 mL) canola oil

½ cup (125 mL) pecan halves, coarsely chopped

¾ cup (175 mL) Apricot Cashew Spread (see recipe, opposite), divided

1. In a large bowl, combine flour, 1 cup (250 mL) oats, sugar, lemon zest, baking powder, baking soda and salt.
2. In a small bowl, whisk together milk, chia seeds and lemon juice; let stand for 5 minutes to thicken slightly.
3. Whisk oil into milk mixture, then quickly stir into flour mixture. Quickly fold in pecans.
4. Divide batter evenly between muffin cups, using a scant ⅓ cup (75 mL) per muffin. Sprinkle with the remaining oats, dividing evenly.
5. Bake in preheated oven for 25 to 30 minutes or until a tester inserted in the center of a muffin comes out without wet batter clinging to it. Let cool completely in pan on a wire rack.
6. Transfer muffins to an airtight container and store at room temperature for up to 3 days or in the refrigerator for up to 4 days.
7. To serve, split each muffin and spread with a heaping tbsp (15 mL) apricot cashew spread.

tip

Look for white chia seeds to use in baking. Once ground, they are less visible, but still have the health benefits of chia.

variations

Use ground flax seeds (flaxseed meal) instead of chia seeds.

Other nuts, such as walnuts or almonds, would be delicious in place of the pecans.

APRICOT CASHEW SPREAD

RAW CASHEWS ARE the cream cheese of the vegan world, and when combined with sweet, tangy apricots, they make a creamy schmear that's delicious on toast, celery sticks or anywhere you'd use jam.

MAKES ABOUT ¾ CUP (175 ML)

Mini chopper or immersion blender

½ cup (125 mL) raw cashews

Water

½ cup (125 mL) dried apricots

1 tbsp (15 mL) freshly squeezed lemon juice

1. Place cashews in a jar or tub and add enough cool water to cover by 2 inches (5 cm). Soak at room temperature for at least 4 hours or in the refrigerator for up to 4 days. Drain well.
2. Meanwhile, place apricots in a jar or tub and add enough warm water to cover by 1 inch (2.5 cm). Soak for at least 1 hour, until fruit is very soft. Drain well.
3. In the mini chopper or using an immersion blender in a tall cup, purée cashews, apricots, 2 tbsp (30 mL) water and lemon juice until smooth, scraping down the sides of the container as needed.
4. Serve immediately or transfer to a jar or other airtight container and store in the refrigerator for up to 3 weeks.

tips

If your apricots are very soft and moist, you may not need to soak them.

If you have a food processor, it will also work well for step 3.

variation

For a fun twist, try another dried fruit, like dates or raisins, in place of the apricots.

GREEN SMOOTHIES
WITH TURMERIC

IF YOU WANT great skin, feed it leafy greens, packed with vitamin A, vitamin C and iron to help rebuild collagen. Turmeric is a powerful antioxidant and speeds healing. For a complete meal, serve these smoothies with rye toast with almond butter.

MAKES 4 SERVINGS

Blender

2 cups (500 mL) unsweetened plain soy milk

4 cups (1 L) cubed pineapple

8 cups (2 L) lightly packed spinach leaves

6 slices gingerroot

2 tbsp (30 mL) slivered fresh turmeric

1. In blender, in batches as necessary, filling jug no more than two-thirds full, combine soy milk, pineapple, spinach, ginger and turmeric; purée to your desired consistency, scraping down the sides of the container as needed. Serve immediately.

tips

Look for fresh turmeric in natural foods stores or Indian groceries. It freezes well, sliced and tightly wrapped.

When making smoothies, place the ingredients in the blender in the order given, with the liquid ingredients first. This will allow the blender to work most effectively.

variation

For even more green power, try hearty greens like Swiss chard or kale in place of the spinach.

SWEET POTATO CHICKPEA CAKES

THESE DELICATE CAKES will take the place of sausage patties without pretending to be meat. Chunky chickpeas and tender sweet potato combine with earthy sage for a fragrant, satisfying breakfast. They're delicious with a yogurt dip, or with your favorite hot sauce, vegan mayo or even ketchup.

MAKES 4 SERVINGS (8 CAKES) | Preheat oven to 250°F (120°C)

1½ cups (375 mL) cooked chickpeas (see page 55), mashed with a fork

1 cup (250 mL) mashed baked sweet potato (see page 45)

½ cup (125 mL) fresh whole wheat bread crumbs

2 tbsp (30 mL) ground flax seeds (flaxseed meal)

2 tsp (10 mL) dried sage, rosemary or thyme

½ tsp (2 mL) salt

½ tsp (2 mL) freshly ground black pepper

Canola oil (see tip)

1 cup (250 mL) plain soy yogurt

tips

If you don't have cooked chickpeas on hand, you can use a 14-oz (398 mL) can, drained and rinsed (or measure 1½ cups/375 mL rinsed drained chickpeas from a larger can).

The amount of oil you need depends on your pan and your tastes. A nonstick pan needs just a smear of oil, although the sides of the cakes will not get browned. A stainless steel or cast-iron pan will require a few tbsp (45 to 60 mL) of oil to keep the cakes from sticking.

1. In a medium bowl, combine chickpeas and sweet potato. There should be rough chunks of chickpeas throughout the mixture. Add bread crumbs, flax seeds, sage, salt and pepper, mixing well.

2. Scoop up ¼-cup (60 mL) portions and place them on a plate. Form each into a 3-inch (7.5 cm) diameter, ¾-inch (2 cm) thick cake. (At this point, they can be covered tightly and refrigerated for up to 1 day.)

3. In a large skillet, heat oil over medium-high heat until shimmering. Working in batches, carefully slip some of the cakes into the pan, leaving 1 inch (2.5 cm) between them. When the oil is sizzling around them, reduce heat to medium and cook for about 4 minutes per side, occasionally using your spatula to carefully lift each cake, preventing it from sticking to the pan. When the cakes are golden brown on the bottom, turn them over and cook for 4 to 5 minutes or until golden brown on the other side. Carefully transfer cakes to a plate lined with paper towels and keep warm in preheated oven. Repeat with the remaining cakes, adding more oil and adjusting heat as necessary between batches. Serve hot, with yogurt for dipping.

PEANUT BUTTER AND CHOCOLATE SMOOTHIES

THE IRRESISTIBLE COMBINATION of peanut butter and chocolate will make this your favorite smoothie. It's also a protein-packed breakfast, and there is even some secret spinach in the mix, so you're getting a veggie!

MAKES 4 SERVINGS

Blender

3 cups (750 mL) unsweetened plain soy milk

2 cups (500 mL) vanilla-flavored soy yogurt

1 cup (250 mL) natural peanut butter (smooth or crunchy)

2 frozen bananas

2 tbsp (30 mL) unsweetened cocoa powder

2 tbsp (30 mL) nutritional yeast

4 cups (1 L) packed baby spinach

2 cups (500 mL) ice cubes

1. In blender, in batches as necessary, filling jug no more than two-thirds full, combine soy milk, yogurt, peanut butter, bananas, cocoa, yeast, spinach and ice cubes; blend to your desired consistency, scraping down the sides of the container as needed. Serve immediately.

tips

Look for light soy milk if you want to cut a few calories.

Nutritional yeast is a great way to add vitamin B_{12} and some extra protein. Try it in other smoothies too!

When making smoothies, place the ingredients in the blender in the order given, with the liquid ingredients first. This will allow the blender to work most effectively.

BREAKFAST PROTEIN COOKIES
WITH DATES AND PISTACHIOS

COOKIES FOR BREAKFAST? Yes, please! It may feel like you're misbehaving, but these whole-grain treats are a respectable meal, thanks to a secret ingredient. Even the pickiest kids will like tofu when it's hidden in a cookie. Serve 3 cookies per serving for breakfast and save the rest for a snack later in the week.

MAKES 14 COOKIES | Preheat oven to 350°F (180°C)

Mini chopper or immersion blender

Large baking sheet, lined with parchment paper

1 cup (250 mL) whole wheat pastry flour

1 cup (250 mL) large-flake (old-fashioned) rolled oats

2 tsp (10 mL) ground cinnamon

1 tsp (5 mL) salt

1 tsp (5 mL) baking soda

6 oz (175 g) silken tofu

2 tbsp (30 mL) ground flax seeds (flaxseed meal)

½ cup (125 mL) pure maple syrup

1½ tsp (7 mL) vanilla extract

¾ cup (175 mL) dates, coarsely chopped

¾ cup (175 mL) pistachios, coarsely chopped

1. In a large bowl, combine flour, oats, cinnamon, salt and baking soda.
2. In the mini chopper or using an immersion blender in a tall cup, purée tofu, flax seeds, maple syrup and vanilla until very smooth, scraping down the sides of the container as needed.
3. Scrape tofu mixture into flour mixture and stir to combine. Stir in dates and pistachios.
4. Scoop up scant ¼-cup (60 mL) portions and form into balls. Place 3 inches (7.5 cm) apart on prepared baking sheet. Wet your palm and flatten balls to ½ inch (1 cm) thick.
5. Bake in preheated oven for 16 minutes, rotating the pan halfway through, until cookies are golden brown and firm. Transfer cookies to wire racks and let cool completely.
6. Store in an airtight container in the refrigerator for up to 1 week.

tips

Silken tofu comes in aseptic boxes, and is shelf-stable until you open it.

If you have a food processor or a high-speed blender, these appliances will also work well for this recipe.

variation

Use half vanilla and half almond extract, and use chopped almonds in place of the pistachios.

BARLEY
WITH VANILLA APPLES AND SPICED SWEET POTATO

IF YOU LOVE pie, this breakfast will make you happy. With a nod to both apple and pumpkin pie, it's a bowl of aromatic and delicious fruits and vegetables, all on a bed of hearty barley.

MAKES 4 SERVINGS

1 cup (250 mL) mashed baked sweet potato (see page 45)

¼ cup (60 mL) nutritional yeast

2 tsp (10 mL) pumpkin pie spice

4 tsp (20 mL) pure maple syrup

3 cups (750 mL) cooked barley (see page 49)

4 Granny Smith apples, peeled and sliced

1 tsp (5 mL) vanilla extract

2 cups (500 mL) plain soy yogurt

½ cup (125 mL) pistachios

1. In a large pot, combine sweet potato, yeast, pumpkin pie spice and maple syrup, stirring until smooth. Stir in barley. Place over medium heat and stir until warmed through. (Alternatively, combine the ingredients in a bowl, then microwave on High for 2 to 3 minutes or until warmed through.)

2. Place apples in a large nonstick skillet over medium heat (see tip). Cook, tossing and stirring, for about 4 minutes or until softened. Stir in vanilla.

3. Divide barley mixture among four bowls, top with yogurt, then apples, and sprinkle with pistachios. Serve warm.

tips

With a good nonstick skillet, you can cook the apples with no oil. If you want to use a cast-iron or stainless steel pan, use a little canola oil to keep them from sticking.

If desired, serve topped with chopped nuts or yogurt and drizzled with additional maple syrup.

Other cooked grains are also delicious prepared this way, especially oat groats, wheat berries and brown rice.

CORNBREAD TOFU SCRAMBLE

ONCE YOU'VE MADE golden cornbread, you'll want to eat it all day long. In this crave-worthy breakfast, cornbread gives your tofu scramble a bit of texture, with that hint of crunch from cornmeal. Serve with more cornbread, if desired.

MAKES 4 SERVINGS

12 oz (375 g) water-packed extra-firm tofu

½ cup (125 mL) chopped cabbage

½ cup (125 mL) frozen corn kernels, thawed

¼ cup (60 mL) nutritional yeast

1 tsp (5 mL) dried sage, crumbled

1 tsp (5 mL) dried thyme

½ tsp (2 mL) ground turmeric

½ tsp (2 mL) salt

Freshly ground black pepper

2 tsp (10 mL) Dijon mustard

1 tsp (5 mL) freshly squeezed lemon juice

2 squares Sweet Potato Cornbread (page 43)

Canola oil

1. Drain tofu and wrap in a clean kitchen towel, pressing lightly to extract as much water as possible.
2. Crumble tofu into a large bowl and, using your hands, mix in cabbage, corn, yeast, sage, thyme, turmeric, salt, pepper to taste, mustard and lemon juice. Do not mash too thoroughly. Crumble in cornbread.
3. Place a large skillet over medium-high heat and let it get hot for about a minute, then drizzle in a little oil. Add tofu mixture and cook, scraping the bottom of the pan every minute or so, until starting to sizzle. Reduce heat to medium and cook, stirring and scraping, for about 5 minutes or until toasty and golden.

tip

Crumbling the tofu with your hands is the best way to get a good texture that resembles the curds of scrambled eggs (but is firmer).

variation

For a curry variation on your scramble, switch the sage and thyme to ground cumin and coriander.

GREEN ALMOND PROTEIN SMOOTHIES

DID YOU KNOW that spinach actually contains protein, despite being low in calories? The spinach in a serving of this smoothie contributes about 1.5 grams of protein and only 10 calories. The almond butter adds about 3 grams of protein and 100 calories. Almond butter is also very nutrient-dense, with healthy fats, calcium and iron. Filling out the protein roster, the yogurt here adds about 4.5 grams, and even the bananas and strawberries contribute a little bit.

MAKES 4 SERVINGS

Blender

2 cups (500 mL) plain soy yogurt

6 cups (1.5 L) lightly packed spinach leaves

2 frozen large bananas, broken into chunks

4 cups (1 L) frozen strawberries

¼ cup (60 mL) almond butter

½ tsp (2 mL) almond extract

1. In blender, in batches as necessary, filling jug no more than two-thirds full, combine yogurt, spinach, banana, strawberries, almond butter and almond extract; blend to your desired consistency, scraping down the sides of the container as needed. Serve immediately.

tips

When the bananas sitting on your counter get ripe and speckled with brown, peel them, put them in zip-top bags and freeze them for use in smoothies and banana bread.

In a pinch, natural peanut butter or another nut butter can fill in for almond butter.

When making smoothies, place the ingredients in the blender in the order given, with the liquid ingredients first. This will allow the blender to work most effectively.

SWEET POTATO SPICE SMOOTHIE BOWLS
WITH SESAME QUINOA

IN FALL AND winter, sweet potatoes and apples are in season, and eating in season is a good way to feel more balanced. This yummy bowl, topped with sweetened quinoa, will remind you of sweet potato pie.

MAKES 4 SERVINGS

Blender

4 medium apples

2 cups (500 mL) unsweetened plain soy milk

2 cups (500 mL) mashed baked sweet potato (see page 45)

¼ cup (60 mL) ground flax seeds (flaxseed meal)

2 tsp (10 mL) ground cinnamon

1 tsp (5 mL) ground allspice

2 cups (500 mL) cooked quinoa (see page 51)

¼ cup (60 mL) toasted sesame seeds (see tip)

4 tsp (20 mL) pure maple syrup

1. Core apples. Cut 16 thin slices from one apple and set aside. Coarsely chop the rest of that apple and the remaining apples.
2. In blender, in batches as necessary, filling jug no more than two-thirds full, combine milk, chopped apples, sweet potato, flax seeds, cinnamon and allspice; purée into a thick smoothie, scraping down the sides of the container as needed.
3. In a small bowl, combine quinoa, sesame seeds and maple syrup.
4. Divide smoothie among four bowls. Pile quinoa mixture in the middle of each bowl. Garnish with apple slices.

tips

Use "eating" apples like Fuji or Gala for this, not baking apples like Granny Smith. Eating apples are sweeter.

To toast sesame seeds, place them in a small dry skillet over medium heat and swirl until fragrant and toasted, about 3 minutes. Spread out on a plate and let cool.

When making smoothies, place the ingredients in the blender in the order given, with the liquid ingredients first. This will allow the blender to work most effectively.

variation

You can use canned pumpkin purée (not pie filling) in place of the sweet potato, but the smoothie will be less sweet.

PEACH POWER SMOOTHIES

SWEET PEACHES AND banana create a soothing backdrop for sprightly parsley, hemp seeds and chia seeds. Parsley is more than just a garnish; it's a potent anticancer, antioxidant green with plenty of vitamins C, A and K to promote optimum well-being. For a complete meal, serve these smoothies with whole wheat toast with peanut butter.

MAKES 4 SERVINGS

Blender

2 cups (500 mL) unsweetened plain soy milk

2 cups (500 mL) lightly packed fresh parsley (stems and leaves)

¼ cup (60 mL) hemp seeds

2 tbsp (30 mL) chia seeds

2 frozen large bananas, broken into chunks

2 cups (500 mL) frozen peach slices

1. In blender, in batches as necessary, filling jug no more than two-thirds full, combine milk, parsley, hemp seeds, chia seeds, bananas and peaches; blend to your desired consistency, scraping down the sides of the container as needed. Serve immediately.

tips

Save parsley stems when you are cooking and purée them to make this yummy smoothie.

When making smoothies, place the ingredients in the blender in the order given, with the liquid ingredients first. This will allow the blender to work most effectively.

variation

If parsley is a little too spicy for your palate, try making this smoothie with spinach, then work up to half parsley to see how you like it.

GREEN PAPAYA SMOOTHIES

BEFORE A LONG DAY (or after a workout), you need a boost of protein and some nourishing spinach. Papaya contributes tons of vitamin C and antioxidants, as well as fruity flavor. Serve the smoothies with whole wheat toast with peanut butter for a complete meal.

MAKES 4 SERVINGS

Blender

2 cups (500 mL) unsweetened plain soy milk

½ cup (125 mL) large-flake (old-fashioned) rolled oats

3 cups (750 mL) frozen papaya chunks

8 cups (2 L) lightly packed spinach leaves

¼ cup (60 mL) almond butter

¼ cup (60 mL) pure maple syrup

2 cups (500 mL) ice cubes

1. In blender, in batches as necessary, filling jug no more than two-thirds full, combine milk, oats, papaya, spinach, almond butter, maple syrup and ice cubes; blend to your desired consistency, scraping down the sides of the container as needed. Serve immediately.

tips

When you see a big papaya in the grocery store, buy it, cube it and freeze what you don't want to eat.

When making smoothies, place the ingredients in the blender in the order given, with the liquid ingredients first. This will allow the blender to work most effectively.

variations

Use vanilla-flavored soy milk.

Substitute another nut butter for the almond butter.

BLUEBERRY BREAKFAST SQUARES

IF YOU LIKE throwing a handful of fresh blueberries over your cereal, you will love these squares, packed with everything in a healthy breakfast, from oats to bananas and berries. You'll love them even more when you're running late and need something to grab and go! Serve 2 squares per serving for breakfast and save the rest for snacks or dessert later in the week.

MAKES 16 SQUARES | Preheat oven to 350°F (180°C)

8-inch (20 cm) square baking pan, lined with parchment paper

1 tbsp (15 mL) ground flax seeds (flaxseed meal)

3 tbsp (45 mL) water

2 ripe medium bananas

½ cup (125 mL) packed light brown sugar

1 tsp (5 mL) vanilla extract

1 cup (250 mL) whole wheat pastry flour

1 cup (250 mL) large-flake (old-fashioned) rolled oats

½ tsp (2 mL) baking powder

½ tsp (2 mL) baking soda

½ tsp (2 mL) salt

1 cup (250 mL) blueberries

¼ cup (60 mL) slivered almonds, coarsely chopped

1. In a cup, stir together flax seeds and water; let stand for 5 minutes to thicken.

2. In a medium bowl, mash bananas and brown sugar. Stir in vanilla.

3. In a large bowl, combine flour, oats, baking powder, baking soda and salt.

4. Stir flaxseed mixture into banana mixture, then stir banana mixture into flour mixture.

5. Spread about two-thirds of the batter in prepared pan. Sprinkle with blueberries. Dollop spoonfuls of the remaining batter over berries. Sprinkle with almonds.

6. Bake in preheated oven for about 30 minutes or until golden brown and a tester inserted in the center comes out clean. Let cool in pan on a wire rack, then cut into 16 squares.

7. Wrap tightly or store in an airtight container for up to 1 week. Refrigerate for best results.

tip

Don't use frozen berries for this, as they will be too wet.

variation

Try making these squares with fresh raspberries, or with dried cranberries in the wintertime.

PREP-AHEAD STEEL-CUT OATS
WITH PEARS AND SPICED SQUASH

ONCE YOU TRY this method for cooking steel-cut oats, you'll wonder why anyone does it the old way. Starting the oats the night before gives them all night to soften, so all you have to do is a quick boil in the morning. A topping of pears and squash makes a meal of it.

MAKES 4 SERVINGS

1 cup (250 mL) steel-cut oats

4 cups (1 L) water

2 cups (500 mL) sliced roasted squash (see page 48)

2 large pears, sliced

½ tsp (2 mL) ground cinnamon

1 cup (250 mL) plain soy yogurt

¼ cup (60 mL) chia seeds

4 tsp (20 mL) pure maple syrup

1. In a medium pot, combine oats and water. Bring to a boil over high heat. Cover, reduce the heat so it won't boil over and cook for 1 minute. Turn off the heat and leave the pot, covered, on the stovetop overnight.
2. In the morning, place the pot over high heat and bring to a boil. Boil, stirring often, for 5 minutes or until oats are tender.
3. Meanwhile, warm squash in the microwave, if desired.
4. Divide oats among four bowls and arrange squash and pear slices on top. Sprinkle squash with cinnamon. Dollop yogurt in the center of each bowl, sprinkle with chia seeds and drizzle with maple syrup. Serve immediately.

tips

Soy yogurt offers the most protein of all the nondairy options, but any nondairy yogurt can be substituted in this recipe.

If you have a heavy-bottomed pot, use it to cook these oats; it will hold the heat longer.

variation

Replace the pear with another fruit, such as a peach or apple.

FARRO, BANANA AND PEANUT BUTTER BOWLS

FARRO IS A chewy, nutty whole grain that tastes just as good with peanut butter as it does with garlic and herbs. A farro bowl will fill you up and keep you energized all morning long.

MAKES 4 SERVINGS

¼ cup (60 mL) natural peanut butter (smooth or crunchy)

1 tsp (5 mL) ground cinnamon

1 cup (250 mL) unsweetened plain soy milk

3 cups (750 mL) cooked farro or wheat berries (see page 50)

2 large bananas, sliced

2 tbsp (30 mL) strawberry jam

2 tbsp (30 mL) unsalted roasted peanuts, chopped

1. In a large pot, stir peanut butter, cinnamon and milk until smooth. Stir in farro. Place over medium heat and cook, stirring, until warmed through.
2. Divide farro mixture among four shallow bowls. Arrange banana slices on top. Dollop ½ tbsp (7 mL) jam on top of each and sprinkle with peanuts. Serve warm.

tip

Grain bowls are portable too; just divide the farro mixture among 2-cup (500 mL) food storage tubs, pack a banana to slice over top and refrigerate until time to serve. Enjoy cold or, if desired, microwave as instructed before adding the banana.

variations

Substitute almond butter for the peanut butter and sprinkle with chopped almonds.

Use your favorite flavor of jam in place of strawberry.

MICROWAVE METHOD In a large bowl, stir peanut butter, cinnamon and milk until smooth. Stir in farro. Divide mixture among four shallow bowls and microwave each on High for 3 minutes or until warmed through. Stir well and top as directed.

CREAMY BROWN RICE CEREAL
WITH DATES AND PISTACHIOS

COOKED BROWN RICE doesn't belong only in savory dishes. Here, it's sweetened with dates to become a perfect breakfast. A sprinkling of pistachios adds crunch and color.

MAKES 4 SERVINGS

4 cups (1 L) cooked medium-grain brown rice (see page 53)

1 cup (250 mL) unsweetened plain soy milk

½ tsp (2 mL) vanilla extract

12 large dates, pitted and chopped

1 cup (250 mL) pistachios, chopped

1. In a large food storage tub or bowl, stir together rice, milk and vanilla, mashing the rice a bit to make it creamy. Stir in dates.
2. Divide rice mixture among four bowls and microwave each on High for 2 minutes or until hot. Serve sprinkled with pistachios.

tips

Short-grain rice is perfect for a creamy cereal because it is softer and stickier than long-grain rice.

Soy milk offers the most protein of all the nondairy options, but any nondairy milk can be substituted in this recipe.

variation

In place of the pistachios, try another type of nut, such as walnuts, or even green pumpkin seeds (pepitas).

STOVETOP METHOD In a small saucepan, stir together rice, milk and vanilla, mashing the rice a bit to make it creamy. Stir in dates and cook, stirring, over medium heat until hot. Divide among four bowls and sprinkle with pistachios.

GRANOLA AND SOY YOGURT WITH BERRIES

YOUR HOMEMADE GRANOLA is so fresh and tasty, it turns this simple breakfast into a treat. You can make it the night before and stir it up when it's time to eat. This one can also go with you on the bus or feed the kids in the backseat. At home, serve it with whole wheat toast with peanut butter, for added protein.

MAKES 4 SERVINGS

Four 1-pint (500 mL) mason jars or 2-cup (500 mL) food storage containers

2 cups (500 mL) plain soy yogurt

2 cups (500 mL) berries

2 cups (500 mL) Fruity Low-Fat Granola (page 40)

1. Place ½ cup (125 mL) yogurt in each jar and top with berries, then granola.
2. Serve immediately or cover and refrigerate for up to 4 days. Store the jars upright, to keep the granola dry until you stir it together to eat.

tips

This is a perfect use for your reusable peanut butter jars, or you can use a sturdy canning jar to carry your breakfast, then rinse it out and use it as a drinking glass for the rest of the day.

Soy yogurt offers the most protein of all the nondairy options, but any nondairy yogurt can be substituted in this recipe.

variation

Replace the berries with sliced peaches or plums, or whatever is in season.

TOFU BROWN RICE SCRAMBLE

I USED TO cook at a vegetarian restaurant where we featured a tofu and brown rice scramble. The combination of the soft and chewy scramble with a crisp piece of toast and a drizzle of creamy tahini was a popular favorite, and it's one that I still crave to this day. Sprinkle extra nutritional yeast over top for a deluxe version.

MAKES 4 SERVINGS

12 oz (375 g) water-packed extra-firm tofu

1 cup (250 mL) cooked medium-grain brown rice (see page 53)

½ cup (125 mL) shredded carrot

¼ cup (60 mL) nutritional yeast

2 tsp (10 mL) chopped gingerroot

1 tsp (5 mL) dried basil

½ tsp (2 mL) ground turmeric

Freshly ground black pepper

1 tbsp (15 mL) tamari

2 tsp (10 mL) Dijon mustard

1 tsp (5 mL) unseasoned rice vinegar

Canola oil

½ cup (125 mL) grape tomatoes, halved

1. Drain tofu and wrap in a clean kitchen towel, pressing lightly to extract as much water as possible.
2. Crumble tofu into a large bowl and, using your hands, mix in rice, carrot, yeast, ginger, basil, turmeric, pepper to taste, tamari, mustard and vinegar. Do not mash too thoroughly.
3. Place a large skillet over medium-high heat and let it get hot for about a minute, then drizzle in a little oil. Add tofu mixture and cook, scraping the bottom of the pan every minute or so, until starting to sizzle. Reduce heat to medium and cook, stirring and scraping, for about 5 minutes or until toasty and golden. Stir in tomatoes and cook, stirring, just until heated through.

tips

For ½ cup (125 mL) shredded carrot, you will need ½ large carrot. Shred it using a box grater or other grater.

Serve the scramble with whole wheat toast and tahini. Stir tahini well when you open it, then refrigerate to keep it from separating.

Try stuffing the scramble into warm whole wheat pitas, for a warm and tasty breakfast sandwich.

BLUEBERRY WHOLE-GRAIN PANCAKES
WITH MAPLE AND PECANS

WHEN YOUR BAKING mix is all prepped, you don't have to wait until Sunday morning to make pancakes. If you get your griddle out and set things up a bit the night before, all you have to do is stir the batter and cook the cakes. Your family will be so happy!

MAKES 8 PANCAKES | Preheat oven to 200°F (100°C)

Griddle or large nonstick skillet

1 tbsp (15 mL) ground flax seeds (flaxseed meal)

1½ cups (375 mL) unsweetened plain soy milk

1 tbsp (15 mL) apple cider vinegar

2 cups (500 mL) Whole-Grain Baking Mix (page 41)

Canola oil

½ cup (125 mL) blueberries

½ cup (125 mL) pure maple syrup

½ cup (125 mL) toasted pecan halves (see tip)

tips

To toast pecans, spread them on a baking sheet and bake at 350°F (180°C) for 10 minutes or until fragrant and lightly toasted.

Be patient with pancakes. Keep the heat at medium, or even turn it down to medium-low if the pancakes are browning too quickly.

1. In a cup, stir together flax seeds, milk and vinegar; let stand for 5 minutes to thicken.
2. Place baking mix in a large bowl and stir in milk mixture just until combined and a little lumpy.
3. Heat griddle over medium-high heat. When hot, oil griddle lightly, using a wadded paper towel or pastry brush. In batches as necessary, scoop batter by rounded ¼-cup (60 mL) portions onto griddle, leaving space for them to spread a little. Reduce heat to medium. Sprinkle a few blueberries on each cake and tap gently with your spatula to press down. Cook until tops of pancakes are covered with bubbles and edges look dry, about 3 minutes. Flip pancakes and cook for about 1 minute or until golden. Transfer pancakes to a plate and keep warm in preheated oven. Repeat with the remaining batter, oiling griddle as needed between batches.
4. Serve hot, with maple syrup and toasted pecans.

variation

Use raspberries, small blackberries or chopped bananas instead of the blueberries.

SWEET POTATO BOWLS
WITH GREENS AND MAPLE PEANUT SAUCE

A SWEET POTATO packs so much sweetness it seems like dessert, but that sweetness masks a nutritious, fiber-rich veggie that even low-carb diners appreciate. Here, it takes a spot usually reserved for grains, to great effect.

MAKES 4 SERVINGS

4 cups (1 L) coarsely chopped baked sweet potatoes (see page 45)

1 tsp (5 mL) extra virgin olive oil

8 large kale leaves, tough stems and center ribs removed

½ cup (125 mL) ready-to-use vegetable broth or Homemade Veggie Stock (page 59)

¼ cup (60 mL) natural peanut butter (smooth or crunchy)

1 tbsp (15 mL) pure maple syrup

1 tbsp (15 mL) tamari

½ tsp (2 mL) freshly ground black pepper

½ tsp (2 mL) ground cinnamon

¼ tsp (1 mL) ground turmeric

½ cup (125 mL) chia seeds

1. Place sweet potatoes in a microwave-safe container and microwave on High for 4 minutes or until warmed through. (Or spread out on a baking sheet and heat in a 400°F/200°C oven for about 20 minutes or until warmed through.)

2. In a large skillet, heat oil over medium-high heat. Add kale and cook, stirring, until tender. Remove from heat.

3. In a small pot, whisk together broth, peanut butter, maple syrup and tamari until smooth. Whisk in pepper, cinnamon and turmeric. Bring to a boil over medium-high heat. Reduce heat and simmer for about 2 minutes or until thickened.

4. Divide sweet potatoes among four bowls. Top with kale, drizzle with peanut sauce and sprinkle with chia seeds.

tip

A bunch of kale ranges from 8 to 16 oz (250 to 500 g), or 8 to 12 large leaves. You may have a few leaves left over for another dish.

variation

Try collard greens in place of kale. Sauté them just a bit longer.

LUNCHES

ROASTED VEGETABLE AND CHICKPEA PAN BAGNAT

THE PAN BAGNAT is traditionally stuffed with tuna, doused in vinaigrette and placed under a weight to marinate the bread in the juices. It's just as delicious made with chickpeas and veggies, speckled with tangy olives.

MAKES 4 SERVINGS

Four 6-inch (15 cm) baguette pieces or hoagie buns

1 cup (250 mL) cooked chickpeas (see page 55)

2 cups (500 mL) roasted broccoli and onion (see page 47)

2 tsp (10 mL) balsamic vinegar

¼ cup (60 mL) packed fresh basil leaves, chopped

¼ cup (60 mL) drained kalamata olives, pitted and chopped

½ tsp (2 mL) salt

½ tsp (2 mL) freshly ground black pepper

2 tsp (10 mL) Dijon mustard

1. Split baguette pieces or buns in half and tear out some of the center of each to make a trough for the filling.
2. Place chickpeas in a large bowl and coarsely mash with a fork or potato masher, just to break them up. Add broccoli and onion. Drizzle with vinegar, then add basil, olives, salt, pepper and mustard, mixing well.
3. Stuff sandwiches with chickpea mixture and wrap each tightly in plastic wrap or waxed paper. Place a cutting board on top of the sandwiches to press them down. Let stand for 10 to 20 minutes under the weight, then refrigerate for at least 1 hour or up to 1 day before serving.

tips

The pan bagnat is meant to be pressed so the filling compresses and the flavorful juices moisten the bread, making mayo or other spreads unnecessary.

Save the bread you remove in step 1 and use it to make bread crumbs for use in other recipes.

variation

Add a chopped roasted red pepper to the filling.

QUINOA BOWLS
WITH KALE AND EDAMAME

BUILD A BOWL and you are good to go for lunch. Packed in a tub, the pickled onion will soften and mellow by lunchtime. If making ahead, slice the avocado at the last minute so it will stay nice and green.

MAKES 4 SERVINGS

1 cup (250 mL) slivered red onion

2 tbsp (30 mL) granulated sugar

2 tbsp (30 mL) apple cider vinegar

½ cup (125 mL) Sesame-Miso Garlic Dressing (page 163)

1 tbsp (15 mL) Sriracha

3 cups (750 mL) cooked quinoa (see page 51)

1 avocado, sliced

4 oz (125 g) baby kale, chopped

2 cups (500 mL) frozen shelled edamame, thawed

1 cup (250 mL) drained roasted red peppers, slivered

1 cup (250 mL) pea sprouts (optional)

1. Place onion in a medium bowl. Add sugar and vinegar, tossing to coat. Let stand at room temperature, stirring occasionally, for at least 10 minutes or up to 1 hour.
2. In a medium bowl or cup, stir together sesame-miso dressing and Sriracha.
3. Divide quinoa among four wide pasta bowls. Arrange pickled onion, avocado, kale, edamame, red peppers and pea sprouts (if using) on top, dividing evenly. Drizzle with dressing.

tips

If you prefer a hot lunch, you can reheat the quinoa (see tip, page 51) before building the bowls.

Quick-pickled red onion gets better with time, so if you have an hour to let it sit and mellow, do so.

variation

Use another flavorful sprout, such as daikon or broccoli, in place of the pea sprouts.

to pack for lunch

Build each bowl in a 3-cup (750 mL) food storage container, omitting the avocado and dressing. Divide dressing among 4 small airtight containers. Refrigerate for up to 1 day. In the morning, pit the avocado, cut it into quarters and sprinkle each with a few drops of apple cider vinegar; wrap each quarter tightly with plastic wrap. Refrigerate until serving. Pack an avocado quarter and a container of dressing along with each bowl. Slice and scoop avocado into the bowl and drizzle with dressing just before serving.

SWEET POTATO HUMMUS
WITH PITAS AND CUCUMBERS

HUMMUS IS ALWAYS great, and this version is a vegetable-infused delight. Deep orange sweet potatoes give it a warm glow, a hint of sweetness and some extra nutrition in every scoop.

MAKES 4 SERVINGS, PLUS LEFTOVER HUMMUS

Immersion blender

2 cloves garlic, chopped

1½ cups (375 mL) cooked chickpeas (see page 55)

1 cup (250 mL) mashed baked sweet potato (see page 45)

¾ cup (175 mL) tahini

½ cup (125 mL) freshly squeezed lemon juice

1 tsp (5 mL) salt (or to taste)

Chopped fresh parsley

Extra virgin olive oil

Four 8-inch (20 cm) whole wheat pitas, cut into wedges

1 cucumber, sliced

1. Using the immersion blender in a tall cup, purée garlic, chickpeas, sweet potato, tahini, lemon juice and salt until smooth.
2. Transfer 1 cup (250 mL) hummus to a food storage container and refrigerate for up to 3 days to enjoy as a snack. Transfer the remaining hummus to a bowl, garnish with parsley and drizzle with oil. Serve with pita wedges (see tip) and cucumber slices.

tips

Adding sweet potatoes to your hummus makes it sweeter, and also adds vegetables to your meal.

This recipe makes about 3 cups (750 mL) hummus. Serve ½ cup (125 mL) per person for lunch and save the rest for snacks.

If desired, brush pita wedges with extra virgin olive oil and toast in a skillet over medium heat or on a rimmed baking sheet in a 350°F (180°C) oven just before serving.

variation

Serve the hummus with whole-grain crackers in place of the pita wedges.

to pack for lunch

After step 1, divide hummus among six 1-cup (250 mL) food storage containers. Garnish with parsley and drizzle with olive oil. Refrigerate for up to 3 days. Pack pita wedges and cucumber slices separately in sandwich bags.

QUINOA TABBOULEH
WITH OLIVES

QUINOA MAKES TERRIFIC tabbouleh, and it's gluten-free, so you can share it with your GF friends. Adding chickpeas bumps up the protein and gives it a lively textural contrast. Olives add a tangy little burst in every bite.

MAKES 4 SERVINGS

8 kalamata olives, pitted and chopped

2 green onions, chopped

1 cucumber, seeded (see tip) and chopped

1 tomato, chopped

1 green bell pepper, chopped

3 cups (750 mL) cooked quinoa (see page 51)

2 cups (500 mL) cooked chickpeas (see page 55)

1 cup (250 mL) packed fresh parsley leaves, minced

½ cup (125 mL) packed fresh mint leaves, minced

DRESSING

2 cloves garlic, minced

¾ tsp (3 mL) salt

½ tsp (2 mL) freshly ground black pepper

¼ cup (60 mL) freshly squeezed lemon juice

¼ cup (60 mL) extra virgin olive oil

1. In a large bowl, combine olives, green onions, cucumber, tomato, green pepper, quinoa, chickpeas, parsley and mint.
2. **DRESSING:** In a cup, stir together garlic, salt, pepper, lemon juice and oil.
3. Pour dressing over quinoa mixture and stir to combine. Serve immediately or transfer to an 8-cup (2 L) food storage tub and refrigerate for up to 3 days.

tips

After peeling and halving the cucumber, use a small spoon to scoop out all the seeds and pulp, because they will make the tabbouleh watery as it sits.

Use a different color bell pepper each time you make this, for variety.

variation

For a little spice, add a minced jalapeño pepper.

to pack for lunch

Divide tabbouleh among four 2-cup (500 mL) food storage containers.

BIG WRAPS
WITH CARROTS, EDAMAME AND SPINACH

WHEN IT COMES to packing a lunch, nothing works quite as well as a wrap. You need the big 10-inch (25 cm) tortillas to contain all the veggies in this delicious roll. The expanse of whole wheat tortilla cradles a rainbow of flavors and colors, all tucked in snugly for your lunchtime enjoyment.

MAKES 4 SERVINGS

4 oz (125 g) dry-packed sun-dried tomatoes (about 1 cup/250 mL)

Hot water

2 cups (500 mL) shredded carrots (see tip)

2 cups (500 mL) frozen shelled edamame, thawed

1 cup (250 mL) Sesame-Miso Garlic Dressing (page 163)

Four 10-inch (25 cm) whole wheat tortillas

4 cups (1 L) lightly packed spinach leaves, chopped

1. Place sun-dried tomatoes in a medium bowl and add enough hot water to cover; let soak for about 10 minutes or until softened, then wring out, chop and return to bowl.
2. Add carrots and edamame to tomatoes. Add dressing, tossing to coat.
3. Place tortillas on a work surface and place one-quarter of the spinach in the center of each, forming a rectangle that extends to 2 inches (5 cm) from either end. Cover spinach with edamame mixture, dividing evenly. Fold in ends and roll up tortillas. Serve immediately.

tips

Sun-dried tomatoes give you a concentrated tomato punch without all the juiciness of fresh tomatoes, which can make your wrap soggy.

For 2 cups (500 mL) shredded carrots, you will need 2 large carrots. Shred them using a box grater or other grater.

variation

Instead of spinach, use finely shredded cabbage.

to pack for lunch

Place wraps, seam side down, in an airtight container or wrap each tightly in waxed paper or plastic wrap. Refrigerate for up to 1 day.

BLUEBERRY BLACK RICE SALAD WITH RADISHES AND MINT

BLACK RICE IS especially beautiful in a salad, providing a dramatic backdrop for the colorful veggies and fruit. I love the juicy berries and the spicy sparkle of radishes in this one, accented by fragrant mint and crunchy walnuts.

MAKES 4 SERVINGS

SALAD

3 large red radishes, diced

2 green onions, chopped

2 cups (500 mL) cooked black rice (see page 52)

1½ cups (375 mL) blueberries

½ cup (125 mL) packed fresh parsley leaves, chopped

½ cup (125 mL) packed fresh mint leaves, chopped

1 cup (250 mL) walnut halves, chopped

Fresh mint sprigs

DRESSING

1 tbsp (15 mL) packed light brown sugar

½ tsp (2 mL) salt

½ tsp (2 mL) freshly ground black pepper

1 tbsp (15 mL) apple cider vinegar

1 tbsp (15 mL) canola oil

1. **SALAD:** In a large bowl, combine radishes, green onions, rice, blueberries, parsley and chopped mint.
2. **DRESSING:** In a cup, whisk together brown sugar, salt, pepper, vinegar and oil.
3. Pour dressing over salad and toss to combine. Serve garnished with walnuts and mint sprigs.

to pack for lunch

Divide dressed salad among four 2-cup (500 mL) food storage containers and top each with 2 tbsp (30 mL) walnuts. Tuck in a mint sprig. Refrigerate for up to 3 days.

TEMPEH BANH MI

BANH MI IS the love child of French and Vietnamese cuisines, and it has taken the world by storm. Something about the quick pickled daikon and carrots combined with the fresh herbs and soy-basted tempeh just makes other sandwiches seem boring.

MAKES 4 SERVINGS | Preheat broiler, with rack set 6 inches (15 cm) from the heat

Four 6-inch (15 cm) baguette pieces, split

Vegan mayonnaise, such as Aquafaba Mayo (page 68)

½ cup (125 mL) finely julienned daikon radish (see tip)

½ cup (125 mL) shredded carrot (see tip)

1 tbsp (15 mL) granulated sugar

¼ tsp (1 mL) salt

2 tbsp (30 mL) unseasoned rice vinegar

16 slices Baked Marinated Tempeh (page 57)

½ cucumber, peeled and sliced

¼ cup (60 mL) packed fresh cilantro leaves

1 red Fresno chile pepper or jalapeño pepper, sliced

2 green onions, sliced on a diagonal

1. Spread cut halves of baguette pieces with mayo; set aside.
2. In a small bowl, combine daikon, carrot, sugar, salt and vinegar. Let stand for 10 minutes.
3. Meanwhile, in a skillet over medium heat, warm tempeh, turning once, for 1 to 2 minutes or until heated through. (Or transfer tempeh to a microwave-safe plate and microwave on High for 1 minute.)
4. Place baguette pieces, cut side up, on a baking sheet. Broil for about 1 minute or until mayo is bubbly and browned in spots.
5. Place the bottom half of each baguette piece on a plate and layer on, in this order, cucumber, tempeh, daikon mixture, cilantro, chile pepper and green onions. Cover each with the top half of the baguette. Serve immediately.

tips

Daikon is a large radish, often over a foot (30 cm) long, so ask your grocer if you can buy a smaller piece. They can cut one in half for you.

To julienne the daikon, cut thin diagonal rounds from the peeled radish and stack them on the cutting board about 3 slices high, then cut into matchsticks.

For ½ cup (125 mL) shredded carrot, you will need ½ large carrot. Shred it using a box grater or other grater.

variations

Replace the tempeh with Baked Marinated Tofu (page 56).

Use red radishes in place of daikon.

to pack for lunch

Skip steps 3 and 4. Assemble the sandwiches as in step 5, but without adding the daikon mixture. Wrap sandwiches in waxed paper or plastic wrap. Divide daikon mixture among 4 small airtight containers. Refrigerate for up to 1 day. Add daikon mixture to each sandwich just before serving.

TOFU SANDWICHES
WITH TOMATOES, LETTUCE AND AVOCADO

IT'S A T-L-T, with chewy marinated tofu at the heart of the sandwich. Marinated tofu makes the best sandwiches — something about the dense, chewy texture and the flavorful crust is just so satisfying. A few slices of avocado are even better than mayonnaise, adding creaminess and that avocado magic we all love.

MAKES 4 SERVINGS

Four 6-inch (15 cm) baguette pieces

1 avocado, sliced

Hot pepper sauce

12 slices Baked Marinated Tofu (page 56)

1 tomato, sliced

4 leaves romaine lettuce

4 tsp (20 mL) Dijon mustard

1. Split baguette pieces in half and tear out some of the center of each to make a trough for the filling.
2. Place avocado slices on bottom halves of baguette and mash lightly. Sprinkle with hot pepper sauce to taste. Cover with tofu, then tomato and romaine. Spread mustard over cut sides of top halves of baguette and close sandwiches.
3. Secure with toothpicks and serve, or wrap tightly and refrigerate overnight.

tip

To slice an avocado, halve the avocado lengthwise and use a chef's knife to pry out the pit, then use the tip of a paring knife to slice the avocado thinly in the shell. Use a small spoon to scoop out the slices.

variation

For chewier sandwiches, replace the tofu with Baked Marinated Tempeh (page 57).

KOREAN MOCK DUCK LETTUCE WRAPS
WITH BLACK RICE

THE LETTUCE WRAP is a fun food. Tender little lettuce leaves serve as edible cups for the intensely flavorful filling, providing a counterpoint in every bite. They also add a bit of salad while acting as a conveyance for all the good food inside.

MAKES 4 SERVINGS

Two 10-oz (284 g) cans mock duck, drained and torn into small pieces

4 green onions, chopped

2 cloves garlic, chopped

1 tsp (5 mL) granulated sugar

1 tbsp (15 mL) tamari

1 tsp (5 mL) toasted (dark) sesame oil

1 tsp (5 mL) gochujang or Sriracha

2 heads Bibb or butter lettuce, leaves separated

2 cups (500 mL) cooked black rice (see page 52), reheated

1 cup (250 mL) drained kimchi

1. In a large bowl, toss together mock duck, green onions, garlic, sugar, tamari, sesame oil and gochujang.

2. Place a large nonstick or cast-iron skillet over medium-high heat. Add mock duck mixture and cook, stirring, until heated through.

3. Arrange lettuce leaves on plates and fill each with a spoonful of rice, mock duck mixture and kimchi. To eat, wrap lettuce over the filling like making a tiny taco.

tips

Gochujang is the fermented, sweet hot sauce of Korea, and Korean fusion has brought it to many mainstream grocery stores. If you can't find it, Sriracha will do.

Other types of lettuce, such as small romaine leaves or radicchio, can also be used.

to pack for lunch

After step 1, divide black rice, mock duck mixture and kimchi among four 2-cup (500 mL) food storage containers. Pack lettuce leaves in separate containers or sealable plastic bags. Refrigerate for up to 1 day. Assemble the lettuce wraps just before serving.

TEMPEH REUBENS ON RYE

THE REUBEN HAS always been a brilliant way to amp up the flavor of a sandwich in one easy step: adding sauerkraut provides instant complexity and a tangy wake-up for your taste buds. We now appreciate it even more because live, naturally fermented kraut is a great source of probiotic bacteria. That's a win-win! For a great accompaniment, serve Arugula Salad (page 158) with Basil Vinaigrette (page 162) alongside these sandwiches.

MAKES 4 SERVINGS

48 slices Baked Marinated Tempeh (page 57)

¼ cup (60 mL) vegan mayonnaise, such as Aquafaba Mayo (page 68)

2 tbsp (30 mL) ketchup

1 tbsp (15 mL) minced sweet pickle or relish

8 slices rye bread, toasted

4 slices red onion

1 avocado, thinly sliced (optional)

1 cup (250 mL) drained sauerkraut

tips

To slice an avocado, halve the avocado lengthwise and use a chef's knife to pry out the pit, then use the tip of a paring knife to slice the avocado thinly in the shell. Use a small spoon to scoop out the slices.

Look for live-fermented kraut, which contains beneficial bacteria, in the refrigerated section of the grocery store. Drain it in a fine-mesh sieve, pressing out the liquid, and pour the liquid back into the jar to cover the remaining kraut.

1. In a skillet over medium heat, in batches as necessary, warm tempeh, turning once, for 1 to 2 minutes or until heated through. (Or transfer tempeh to a microwave-safe plate and microwave on High for 1 minute.)
2. In a small bowl, stir together mayo, ketchup and pickle. Spread mixture over 4 bread slices, dividing evenly, then layer on tempeh, red onion, avocado (if using) and sauerkraut. Place the remaining bread slices on top.

variation

If you like a little spice in your sandwich, use kimchi instead of sauerkraut.

to pack for lunch

Skip toasting the bread, and skip step 1. Assemble the sandwiches as in step 2, but without adding the avocado or sauerkraut. Wrap sandwiches in waxed paper or plastic wrap. Divide sauerkraut among 4 small airtight containers. Refrigerate for up to 1 day. If using avocado, in the morning, pit it, cut it into quarters and sprinkle each with a few drops of lemon juice; wrap each quarter tightly with plastic wrap. Refrigerate until serving. Just before serving, slice avocado and add to the sandwich, along with the sauerkraut.

BLACK BEAN NACHOS
WITH OLIVES

I'VE NEVER TRIED the nachos they sell at the gas station, where you can pump hot orange goo over a paper tray of chips, but somebody out there loves it. Forget that junk food. This packable vegan version has a creamy, spicy sauce based on cashews and other healthy plants. If you have a microwave at work, you can have a plateful of enviable nachos in minutes.

MAKES 4 SERVINGS

½ cup (125 mL) cherry tomatoes, chopped

¼ cup (60 mL) drained kalamata olives, pitted and chopped

1 tsp (5 mL) chipotle chile powder

2 cups (500 mL) Creamy Cheesy Sauce (page 62)

4 oz (125 g) tortilla chips (about 60 chips)

1 cup (250 mL) rinsed drained canned black beans

1. In a small saucepan, combine tomatoes, olives, chile powder and cheesy sauce. Cook over medium heat, stirring often, for about 4 minutes or until heated through.
2. Spread tortilla chips over four plates and sprinkle with black beans. Pour hot cheese sauce over top. Serve immediately.

variation

If you are not excited about olives, substitute chopped green onions or jalapeños.

tips

If you happen to have cooked black beans in the fridge or freezer, feel free to use them instead of canned.

Big corn chips are great here, and you can use fat-free baked chips if you are looking to cut back on oil.

to pack for lunch

Combine the ingredients for the nacho sauce in a bowl, then divide among four 1-cup (250 mL) food storage containers; divide beans among four small containers. Refrigerate for up to 2 days. Pack chips separately in small containers. Heat nacho sauce in the microwave on High for 2 minutes, stirring halfway through, then assemble as in step 2.

SHREDDED VEGGIE SALAD WITH PESTO

SOMETIMES YOU JUST want a heartier salad, and shredded cabbage and carrots give this one some gravitas. Unlike leafy green salads, shredded cabbage and carrots actually improve as they sit in a dressing overnight. The cabbage softens slightly, making it a gentle companion to the crunchy seeds.

MAKES 4 SERVINGS

7 cups (1.75 L) Shredded Cabbage and Carrots (page 44)

2 green onions, chopped

½ tsp (2 mL) salt

½ cup (125 mL) Basil Pesto (page 66)

½ cup (125 mL) roasted sunflower seeds

¼ cup (60 mL) green pumpkin seeds (pepitas), toasted (see tip)

1. In a large bowl, combine shredded vegetables and green onions. Sprinkle with salt. Add pesto and toss to coat. Serve sprinkled with sunflower and pumpkin seeds.

variation

For a pretty presentation, use half red and half green cabbage when preparing the shredded cabbage.

tips

Roasted sunflower seeds are sold in the snack nuts section. They can usually be found either salted or unsalted, and either can be used in this recipe, as you prefer. If you use salted sunflower seeds, add only ¼ tsp (1 mL) salt to the recipe and adjust from there. They also make a great packable snack.

Toast pumpkin seeds in a dry skillet over medium heat, stirring constantly, for 3 to 5 minutes or until golden and fragrant. Immediately transfer to a bowl to cool.

to pack for lunch

Divide salad among four 2-cup (500 mL) food storage containers. Refrigerate for up to 3 days. Pack sunflower and pumpkin seeds in a sandwich bag. Sprinkle salad with seeds just before serving.

CHICKPEA SLAW WRAPS
WITH CHEESY SAUCE

WRAP UP AN easy meal, with all your handy prep work combining for maximum effect. Crunchy vegetables, creamy cheesy sauce and juicy tomatoes combine for lunchtime fun. Because you prepped, you can just wrap and go!

MAKES 4 SERVINGS

4 cups (1 L) Shredded Cabbage and Carrots (page 44)

2 cups (500 mL) rinsed drained canned chickpeas

½ tsp (2 mL) salt

1 tbsp (15 mL) Dijon mustard

1 cup (250 mL) Creamy Cauliflower Sauce (page 63)

Four 10-inch (25 cm) whole wheat tortillas

½ cup (125 mL) cherry tomatoes, halved

1. In a large bowl, toss together shredded vegetables, chickpeas, salt and mustard.
2. Spread ¼ cup (60 mL) sauce over each tortilla. Top with one-quarter of the vegetable mixture and cherry tomato halves. Fold in ends and roll up tortillas.
3. If desired, warm wraps in the microwave on High for 2 minutes. (Or place seam side down in a hot skillet over medium-high heat and cook, turning once, for about 3 minutes or until tortilla is crisped on both sides.)

tips

If you happen to have cooked chickpeas in the fridge or freezer, feel free to use them instead of canned.

If you have extra Creamy Cheesy Sauce (page 62) on hand, you can use it in place of the Creamy Cauliflower Sauce.

Large tortillas are needed to hold all the fillings in this wrap. Tortillas freeze well, so keep some in the freezer, and thaw them when you're ready to wrap.

variation

Shred a beet or zucchini in with the other vegetables, for a more colorful mix.

to pack for lunch

Prepare through step 2 and place wraps, seam side down, in an airtight container or wrap each tightly in waxed paper or plastic wrap. Refrigerate for up to 1 day. If desired, warm in the microwave as directed in step 3 before serving.

BARLEY, TOFU BURGER AND BEET BOWLS
WITH BASIL VINAIGRETTE

AREN'T YOU GLAD you have those tofu quinoa burgers in the refrigerator? Slice them over a barley bowl for a sensational lunch. This bowl covers all the bases, with chewy barley, sweet and earthy beets and creamy avocado, all bathed in your freshly made vinaigrette.

MAKES 4 SERVINGS

4 cups (1 L) cooked barley (see page 49)

4 cups (1 L) arugula

1 cup (250 mL) sliced roasted beets (see page 46)

2 green onions, slivered

1 avocado, sliced

½ cup (125 mL) Basil Vinaigrette (page 162)

4 Tofu Quinoa Burgers (page 139), each cut into 4 slices

tips

Barley comes in pearl, pot and hulled forms, and any of these can be used in this recipe, depending on your taste. Pearl barley is softer after cooking, hulled barley retains a little crunch, and pot barley is somewhere in between.

If you have some sauerkraut or kimchi handy, go ahead and garnish each bowl with it.

1. Divide barley among four bowls. Arrange arugula, beets, green onions and avocado on top. Drizzle each with 2 tbsp (30 mL) vinaigrette. Arrange burger slices on top.

to pack for lunch

Divide barley among four 3-cup (750 mL) food storage containers. Arrange arugula, beets, green onions and burgers on top. Divide vinaigrette among 4 small airtight containers. Refrigerate for up to 1 day. In the morning, pit the avocado, cut it into quarters and sprinkle each with a few drops of lemon juice; wrap each quarter tightly with plastic wrap. Refrigerate until serving. Slice and scoop avocado into the bowl and drizzle with vinaigrette just before serving.

AVOCADO GODDESS SALAD WITH EDAMAME

GREEN GODDESS DRESSING is a classic, usually made green by parsley minced into a mayonnaise and sour cream base. Skip all that dairy and go with this creamy avocado version. It's just as luscious, and better for you.

MAKES 4 SERVINGS

Blender

DRESSING

1 avocado

2 cloves garlic, chopped

1 cup (250 mL) packed fresh basil leaves

½ cup (125 mL) packed fresh parsley leaves

½ tsp (2 mL) salt

2 tbsp (30 mL) white wine vinegar

½ cup (125 mL) extra virgin olive oil

SALAD

1 head romaine lettuce, chopped

2 tomatoes, sliced

2 oz (60 g) broccoli sprouts

1 cup (250 mL) frozen shelled edamame, thawed

½ cup (125 mL) pistachios

6 tbsp (90 mL) hemp seeds

tip

This method for making salad dressing — drizzling in the oil with the blender running — is the best way to make a stable emulsion that will not separate.

1. **DRESSING:** Halve the avocado, remove the pit and scoop the flesh from each half out of the shell into the blender. Add garlic, basil, parsley, salt and vinegar. Blend until smooth, scraping down the sides of the container as needed. With the motor running, through the feed tube, drizzle in oil, then blend on high speed for about 5 seconds to a smooth purée.
2. **SALAD:** Place romaine in a large bowl and top with tomatoes, broccoli sprouts and edamame. Drizzle with dressing and toss to coat. Sprinkle with pistachios and hemp seeds. Serve immediately.

variations

Other kinds of greens are delicious in place of the romaine.

If you can't find broccoli sprouts, try alfalfa, daikon or radish sprouts.

to pack for lunch

After step 1, divide dressing among 4 small airtight containers. Divide romaine among four 4-cup (1 L) food storage tubs and top with tomatoes, broccoli sprouts and edamame. Refrigerate for up to 2 days. Pack pistachios and hemp seeds in a sandwich bag. Toss salad with dressing and sprinkle with nuts and seeds just before serving.

CHILE-LIME BLACK BEAN HUMMUS WITH CHIPS AND SALSA

YES, WE LOVE the taste of chickpeas in our hummus, but black beans have their charms as well. They've been carrying refried beans for years, and in this tasty dip, you'll find that the hints of spice and lime are welcome.

MAKES 4 SERVINGS

Mini chopper or immersion blender

3 cloves garlic, chopped

1½ cups (375 mL) cooked black beans (see page 54)

¼ cup (60 mL) ready-to-use vegetable broth, Homemade Veggie Stock (page 59) or water

6 tbsp (90 mL) tahini

6 tbsp (90 mL) freshly squeezed lime juice (see tip)

Extra virgin olive oil

1 tsp (5 mL) salt

½ tsp (2 mL) chipotle chile powder (or to taste)

4 oz (125 g) tortilla chips (about 60 chips)

Tomato Cilantro Salsa (page 65)

1. In the mini chopper or using an immersion blender in a tall cup, purée garlic, beans, broth, tahini, lime juice, 2 tbsp (30 mL) oil, salt and chile powder until smooth, scraping down the container as needed.

2. Transfer hummus to a bowl and drizzle with additional olive oil. Serve with tortilla chips and salsa.

tips

For 6 tbsp (90 mL) lime juice, you will need 3 or 4 limes.

This recipe makes about 2 cups (500 mL) hummus. If your mini chopper holds less than 3 cups (750 mL), you will need to prepare this recipe in batches.

If you have a food processor or a high-speed blender, these appliances will also work well for this recipe. If using the blender, add the broth first, then the other ingredients.

to pack for lunch

After step 1, divide hummus among four 1-cup (250 mL) food storage containers and drizzle with additional olive oil. Refrigerate for up to 3 days. Pack chips in sandwich bags and salsa in small airtight containers.

FARRO AND KIMCHI BOWLS
WITH KALE AND SESAME DRESSING

ROMAN GLADIATORS FILLED their bellies with farro and barley as they marched across the empire. You don't need to conquer the known world quite so literally, but a good grain-based lunch will help you power your way through the day.

MAKES 4 SERVINGS

4 cups (1 L) cooked farro or wheat berries (see page 50)

8 kale leaves, tough stems and center ribs removed, leaves chopped

2 tsp (10 mL) extra virgin olive oil (optional)

1 red bell pepper, sliced

1 cup (250 mL) drained kimchi

½ cup (125 mL) Sesame-Miso Garlic Dressing (page 163)

½ cup (125 mL) roasted cashews

1. Divide farro among four shallow bowls.
2. Use kale raw or, to quickly sauté it, place a large skillet over medium-high heat, drizzle with olive oil, then add kale and cook, stirring, for about 2 minutes or until wilted and slightly crisped. Divide kale among bowls, placing it on one side.

3. Arrange red pepper and kimchi on the other side of the bowls, then drizzle with dressing and sprinkle with cashews.

tip

These bowls are great warm or cold. For a warm bowl, microwave it on High for 2 minutes before adding dressing.

variation

If you aren't a fan of kale, try another green, like spinach or Swiss chard.

to pack for lunch

Divide farro among four 3-cup (750 mL) food storage containers and arrange kale, red pepper and kimchi on top. Refrigerate for up to 2 days. Pack dressing and cashews separately in small containers. Drizzle farro bowls with dressing and sprinkle with cashews just before serving.

BLACK BEAN BURRITOS
WITH SQUASH AND CILANTRO FARRO

IF YOU MISS the way that melty cheese melds burritos together, try using mashed squash instead. It performs the same function, forming a matrix of tasty goodness that holds the beans in place as you take bite after delicious bite.

MAKES 4 SERVINGS

1 cup (250 mL) mashed roasted kabocha or red kuri squash (see page 48)

1 tsp (5 mL) salt

1 tsp (5 mL) chili powder

1 cup (250 mL) cooked farro or wheat berries (see page 50)

¼ cup (60 mL) packed fresh cilantro leaves, chopped

1 tsp (5 mL) extra virgin olive oil

Four 10-inch (25 cm) whole wheat tortillas

1 cup (250 mL) cooked black beans (see page 54)

Pinch salt

Hot pepper sauce

1 cup (250 mL) Tomato Cilantro Salsa (page 65)

1 cup (250 mL) guacamole (see tip)

1 cup (250 mL) soy yogurt

1. In a medium bowl, combine squash, salt and chili powder.
2. In another bowl, combine farro, cilantro and oil.
3. Place tortillas on a work surface and spread one-quarter of the squash mixture in the center of each, forming a rectangle about 2 inches (5 cm) across and 5 inches (12.5 cm) long. Cover squash with farro mixture, then beans, dividing evenly. Sprinkle with salt and hot pepper sauce to taste. Fold in ends and roll up burritos. Serve with salsa, guacamole and yogurt.

tips

Kabocha and red kuri squash provide a meaty texture and deep orange flesh. Butternut, acorn and other squashes are moister and may make your burritos soggy.

If you prefer, you can reheat the farro (see tip, page 50) before assembling the burritos.

To make a quick guacamole, just mash the flesh of an avocado with a few squeezes of fresh lime juice, a pinch of salt and a few chopped cilantro leaves.

to pack for lunch

Place wraps, seam side down, in an airtight container or wrap each tightly in waxed paper or plastic wrap. Refrigerate for up to 1 day. Pack salsa, guacamole and yogurt in small airtight containers.

FARRO SALAD
WITH APRICOTS, CARROT AND SPINACH

THE PAIRING OF chewy, nutty farro and fruit is always a winner, and dried apricots add nuggets of chewy sweetness to this salad. Dried fruit is a great pantry item — you don't have to wait for the moment of perfect ripeness, because perfect ripeness was preserved for you.

MAKES 4 SERVINGS

SALAD

2 green onions, chopped

1 carrot, shredded (see tip)

4 cups (1 L) packed spinach leaves

2 cups (500 mL) cooked farro or wheat berries (see page 50)

½ cup (125 mL) dried apricots, sliced

½ cup (125 mL) sunflower seeds

DRESSING

2 tbsp (30 mL) pure maple syrup

2 tbsp (30 mL) freshly squeezed lemon juice

2 tbsp (30 mL) canola oil

½ tsp (2 mL) ground cinnamon

½ tsp (2 mL) paprika

½ tsp (2 mL) salt

1. **SALAD:** In a large bowl, toss together green onions, carrot, spinach, farro, apricots and sunflower seeds.
2. **DRESSING:** In a small bowl, whisk together maple syrup, lemon juice, oil, cinnamon, paprika and salt.
3. Drizzle dressing over salad and toss to coat.

tips

Shred the carrot using a box grater or other grater.

Spoon your salad into a whole wheat pita for added protein.

variation

Try making the dressing with olive or walnut oil, for a more pronounced flavor.

to pack for lunch

Prepare through step 3 and divide among four 2-cup (500 mL) containers. Refrigerate for up to 1 day. Cooked grains are a little crunchy when chilled, so let the farro come to room temperature before serving, if you can.

SQUASH AND BLACK BEAN ROLL-UPS
WITH SPINACH

THE SPIRAL ROLL is a pretty way to make your lunch. These can be sliced on a diagonal, giving you an Instagram-worthy presentation. They can also be eaten with one hand while you work at your desk, but you know you deserve a moment to enjoy your lunch, right?

MAKES 4 SERVINGS

2 cups (500 mL) cooked black beans (see page 54)

1 cup (250 mL) mashed roasted squash (see page 48)

1 tsp (5 mL) dried oregano

½ tsp (2 mL) salt

Four 10-inch (25 cm) whole wheat tortillas

2 green onions, chopped

2 tomatoes, chopped

4 cups (1 L) packed spinach leaves, chopped

Cholula or other hot pepper sauce

1. In a medium bowl, coarsely mash beans and squash. Add oregano and salt, stirring well.

2. Place tortillas on a work surface and spread one-quarter of the bean mixture over each, covering all but about 1 inch (2.5 cm) along one edge. Sprinkle green onions, tomatoes and spinach over bean mixture. Sprinkle with hot pepper sauce to taste.

3. Roll up tortillas like a cinnamon roll, with the bare edge last. Cut each roll-up in half.

tip

Whole wheat tortillas have more fiber, protein, vitamins and minerals than their white flour counterparts, so stick with whole grains.

variation

For added color, substitute shredded red cabbage for some of the spinach.

to pack for lunch

Before cutting the roll-ups in half, wrap each tightly in waxed paper or plastic wrap. Refrigerate for up to 1 day.

TEMPEH TACOS
WITH MANGO SRIRACHA SAUCE

TACOS! JUST THE word conjures up images of taco trucks and parties al fresco. Take a little of the party to work with these packable flavor bombs filled with smoky, chewy tempeh, crunchy cabbage, creamy avocados and spicy Mango Sriracha Sauce over it all.

MAKES 4 SERVINGS | Preheat oven to 200°F (100°C)

8 hard taco shells or 6-inch (15 cm) corn tortillas

2 cups (500 mL) Smoky Tempeh Taco Meat (page 58)

2 cups (500 mL) shredded red cabbage (see tip)

1 tsp (5 mL) freshly squeezed lime juice

Pinch salt

2 avocados, sliced (see tip, page 110)

1½ cups (375 mL) grape tomatoes, sliced

½ cup (125 mL) Mango Sriracha Sauce (page 64)

1. Wrap taco shells or tortillas in foil and warm in preheated oven for 15 to 20 minutes.
2. Warm taco meat in the microwave on High for 2 minutes. (Or place in a skillet over medium-low heat and cook, stirring, until heated through.)
3. In a medium bowl, toss cabbage with lime juice and salt.
4. Place 2 taco shells on each plate and fill with taco meat, cabbage mixture, avocados and tomatoes, dividing evenly. Drizzle with mango sauce.

variation

Small "soft taco" flour tortillas can also be used, if you prefer wheat to corn.

tip

For 2 cups (500 mL) shredded red cabbage, you'll need about an 8-oz (250 g) wedge of cabbage. Insert the slicing blade into a food processor, put the lid on and have the tamper ready. Cut cabbage into vertical pieces that will fit into the feed tube. With the motor running, drop cabbage into the feed tube. Don't push down with the tamper unless the cabbage becomes lodged in the feed tube — the less pressure you put on the cabbage, the thinner the slices will be. If you don't have a food processor, use a knife to thinly sliver the wedge of cabbage.

to pack for lunch

Skip step 1 and place 2 taco shells or tortillas in each of 4 sealable plastic bags. Divide taco meat among 4 small airtight containers. Prepare cabbage mixture as in step 3 and divide it among four 1-cup (250 mL) containers; place tomatoes and avocados on top and drizzle with an extra squeeze of lime juice and the mango sauce. Refrigerate for up to 1 day. Just before serving, warm the taco meat in the microwave as in step 2, divide it between the shells and top with cabbage mixture.

BROWN RICE BOWLS
WITH ROASTED CARROTS AND MOCK DUCK

PEANUT BUTTER IS a vegan staple, but if you haven't made almond butter part of your life, it's time. In this easy bowl, almond butter transforms into a tangy, umami-rich sauce and also contributes some protein and other great nutrition. Mock duck is a convenient, meaty addition that always goes well with brown rice.

MAKES 4 SERVINGS

SAUCE

2 cloves garlic, minced

½ cup (125 mL) almond butter

¼ cup (60 mL) unsweetened apple juice

2 tbsp (30 mL) tamari

2 tbsp (30 mL) apple cider vinegar

2 tbsp (30 mL) white miso

RICE BOWLS

4 cups (1 L) cooked medium-grain brown rice (see page 53), reheated

4 cups (1 L) packed baby spinach, chopped

2 cups (500 mL) diagonally sliced roasted carrots (see page 47)

Two 10-oz (284 g) cans mock duck, drained and torn into small pieces

Pea shoots (optional)

1. **SAUCE:** In a medium bowl, whisk together garlic, almond butter, apple juice, tamari, vinegar and miso.

2. **RICE BOWLS:** Divide rice among four shallow bowls. Arrange spinach, carrots, mock duck and pea shoots on top. Drizzle each with ¼ cup (60 mL) sauce.

tip

Buy apple juice in single-serving bottles or boxes to use in small amounts for cooking and baking.

variations

Replace the mock duck with 1¼ lbs (625 g) seitan, drained and torn.

For a gluten-free version, use baked tofu or tempeh (store-bought or see recipes, pages 56 and 57) in place of the mock duck.

to pack for lunch

After step 1, divide sauce among 4 small airtight containers. Assemble each rice bowl in a 4-cup (1 L) food storage tub, omitting the sauce. Refrigerate for up to 2 days. Drizzle with sauce just before serving.

SWEET POTATO AND MUMBAI LENTILS
WITH CUCUMBER RAITA

THE DELICIOUS MUMBAI Lentils and Kale you made for dinner goes the extra mile by serving as a topper for these lunch bowls later in the week. Thanks to your prepped sweet potato, you have all you need for a bunch of flavors and textures in one spicy place, and the side of cooling raita complements it all perfectly.

MAKES 4 SERVINGS

¾ cup (175 mL) chopped seeded cucumber

½ tsp (2 mL) salt

½ tsp (2 mL) ground cumin

½ cup (125 mL) soy yogurt

2 tbsp (30 mL) freshly squeezed lemon juice

3 cups (750 mL) sliced baked sweet potato (see page 45), warmed (see tip)

3 cups (750 mL) Mumbai Lentils and Kale (page 149), warmed (see tip)

2 tbsp (30 mL) sesame seeds

1. In a medium bowl, combine cucumber, salt, cumin, yogurt and lemon juice.
2. In each of four bowls, place ¾ cup (175 mL) sweet potato on one side and ¾ cup (175 mL) kale mixture on the other side. Sprinkle with sesame seeds. Serve with raita alongside.

variation

Make the raita with zucchini instead of cucumber.

tips

Warm the sweet potato in the microwave on High for about 3 minutes, or in a skillet on the stovetop over medium-low heat, stirring until heated through.

Warm the Mumbai Lentils and Kale in the microwave on High for about 3 minutes, or in a skillet on the stovetop over medium-low heat, stirring until heated through.

to pack for lunch

After step 1, divide raita among 4 small airtight containers. Refrigerate for up to 2 days. Leave the sweet potato and the kale mixture cold. In each of four 2-cup (500 mL) food storage tubs, place ¾ cup (175 mL) sweet potato on one side and ¾ cup (175 mL) kale mixture on the other side. Sprinkle with sesame seeds and refrigerate until serving. Warm in the microwave on High for 3 minutes just before serving. Serve with cold raita alongside.

TEMPEH, BROWN RICE AND ROASTED VEGGIE WRAPS

YOUR PREP WILL serve you well with this wrap, combining your stashed tempeh, veggies and brown rice with fresh spinach for a satisfying meal. Sriracha mayo gives it a little kick and a little creaminess.

MAKES 4 SERVINGS

24 slices Baked Marinated Tempeh (page 57)

2 cups (500 mL) sliced roasted carrots (see page 47)

½ cup (125 mL) vegan mayonnaise, such as Aquafaba Mayo (page 68)

1 tbsp (15 mL) Sriracha

2 cups (500 mL) packed spinach leaves, coarsely chopped

1 cup (250 mL) sliced baked sweet potato (see page 45)

1 cup (250 mL) cooked medium-grain brown rice (see page 53)

Four 10-inch (25 cm) whole wheat tortillas

1. In a large bowl, combine tempeh and carrots.
2. In a cup, stir together mayo and Sriracha. Drizzle over tempeh mixture.
3. In another large bowl, toss together spinach, sweet potato and rice.
4. Place tortillas on a work surface and place one-quarter of the spinach mixture in the center of each. Top with tempeh mixture, dividing evenly. Fold in ends and roll up tortillas.

tips

If you don't have homemade mayo on hand, try a vegan mayo like Fabanaise or Just Mayo.

If you prefer, you can reheat the rice (see tip, page 53) before step 3.

variation

Substitute shredded kale for the spinach, for more texture and crunch.

to pack for lunch

Place wraps, seam side down, in an airtight container or wrap each tightly in waxed paper or plastic wrap. Refrigerate for up to 1 day.

MEATLOAF SANDWICHES
WITH LETTUCE AND TOMATO

HONESTLY, SOMETIMES I think the meatloaf sandwich is the main reason I make the meatloaf. Your tempeh meatloaf is so flavorful and has so much going on, few other sandwich fillings can compare. Your advance prep work will make you happy today.

MAKES 4 SERVINGS

½ Tempeh Meatloaf (page 150), cut into 4 slices

1 tsp (5 mL) canola oil (optional)

¼ cup (60 mL) vegan mayonnaise, such as Aquafaba Mayo (page 68)

2 tbsp (30 mL) Dijon mustard

8 slices whole wheat bread, toasted

4 lettuce leaves

4 slices tomato

1. Warm meatloaf in the microwave on High for 2 minutes. (Or heat oil in a skillet over medium heat; add meatloaf slices and cook, turning, for about 2 minutes or until heated through.)
2. Spread mayo and mustard over 4 bread slices. Top each with a meatloaf slice, then with lettuce and tomato. Cover with the remaining bread slices. Serve immediately.

tips

You can use frozen meatloaf slices in these sandwiches if preparing them ahead. Just pop a slice into a sandwich the night before and it should be thawed by the time you're ready for lunch.

Try different mustards, like raspberry-flavored or whole-grain, to shake up your sandwich game.

to pack for lunch

Skip step 1 and skip toasting the bread. Assemble the sandwiches as in step 2, wrap tightly and refrigerate for up to 1 day.

DINNERS

week 1

week 2

week 3

week 4

week 5

AVOCADO QUESADILLAS
WITH RASPBERRY SALSA

WHO NEEDS CHEESE when you have creamy avocado to fill your quesadilla? Quesadillas are a cross between a grilled cheese sandwich and a chip for dipping, and are just as delightful filled with luscious avocado. The colorful, tangy salsa is the perfect pairing. Serve the quesadillas with Everyday Green Salad (page 156) with Balsamic Vinaigrette (page 161) on the side.

MAKES 4 SERVINGS

RASPBERRY SALSA

2 kiwifruits, chopped

2 green onions, chopped

1 jalapeño pepper, seeded and minced

1½ cups (375 mL) raspberries

¼ cup (60 mL) packed fresh cilantro leaves, chopped

1 tbsp (15 mL) freshly squeezed lime juice

AVOCADO QUESADILLAS

3 avocados

½ tsp (2 mL) salt

¼ tsp (1 mL) chipotle chile powder

Eight 8-inch (20 cm) whole wheat tortillas

1 cup (250 mL) green pumpkin seeds (pepitas), toasted (see tip)

1. **SALSA:** In a small bowl, combine kiwis, green onions, jalapeño, raspberries, cilantro and lime juice. Set aside.
2. **QUESADILLAS:** In a medium bowl, using a fork, mash avocados. Stir in salt and chile powder.
3. Place 4 of the tortillas on a work surface. Spread one-quarter of the avocado mixture over each tortilla. Top each with another tortilla.
4. Heat a large cast-iron pan or a large skillet over high heat until hot. Slide a quesadilla into the pan and cook for about 2 minutes, turning once, until browned on both sides. Slide quesadilla onto a cutting board and slide the next quesadilla into the pan. Cut the hot one into 6 wedges and transfer to plates. Repeat until all the quesadillas are cooked.
5. Serve quesadillas warm, dolloped with salsa and sprinkled with pumpkin seeds.

tips

Buy big kiwifruits for this recipe or, if you see a bag of small kiwis on sale, use 3 smaller ones. Use the rest of the kiwis to garnish smoothies and smoothie bowls.

Toast pumpkin seeds in a dry skillet over medium heat, stirring constantly, for 3 to 5 minutes or until golden and fragrant. Immediately transfer to a bowl to cool.

variation

For more heat, use a hotter chile, like a serrano or Thai red chile, in place of the jalapeño.

ROASTED VEGETABLE CHICKPEA PENNE
WITH SUN-DRIED TOMATO PESTO

TAKE ADVANTAGE OF the concentrated flavor and umami of sun-dried tomatoes in this easy pasta. Instead of cooking them, you can just hydrate and purée them to a rich, intense sauce. Your prepped vegetables add even more concentrated flavor, giving a simple dish satisfyingly complex flavor. Serve it with Arugula Salad (page 158) with Balsamic Vinaigrette (page 161) on the side.

MAKES 4 SERVINGS

Mini chopper or immersion blender

SUN-DRIED TOMATO PESTO

1 oz (30 g) sun-dried tomatoes (¼ cup/60 mL packed)

Hot water

2 cloves garlic, chopped

½ cup (125 mL) packed fresh parsley leaves

½ tsp (2 mL) salt

¼ cup (60 mL) extra virgin olive oil

ROASTED VEGETABLE CHICKPEA PENNE

8 oz (250 g) dried whole wheat penne pasta

2 cups (500 mL) roasted broccoli and onion (see page 47)

1 cup (250 mL) cooked chickpeas (see page 55)

1. **PESTO:** Place sun-dried tomatoes in a small bowl and add enough hot water to cover; let soak for about 10 minutes or until softened, then drain and wring out.
2. In the mini chopper or using an immersion blender in a tall cup, purée tomatoes, garlic, parsley, salt and oil until fairly smooth, scraping down the sides of the container as needed.
3. **PENNE:** In a large pot of boiling salted water, cook pasta according to package directions until al dente, about 9 minutes. Drain well.
4. Return pasta to the pot and add broccoli, onion, chickpeas and pesto. Cook, stirring, over medium-low heat just until heated through. Serve hot.

tips

When you purchase sun-dried tomatoes, squeeze the package to see if they are flexible. Softer dried tomatoes are easier to work with, and often fresher-tasting.

Place Cashew Parmesan (page 69) on the table for people to sprinkle on top.

If you have a food processor or a high-speed blender, these appliances will also work well for step 2 of this recipe.

variation

If you have fresh basil or arugula available, they make a great replacement for the parsley.

QUINOA CORN CHOWDER

QUINOA IS SO nutty and delicious, and pairing it with sweet, creamy corn takes it over the top. Potatoes give it a little body and thicken the creamy mixture, while red peppers give the soup pops of color. Serve it with Everyday Green Salad (page 156) with Sesame-Miso Garlic Dressing (page 163).

MAKES 4 SERVINGS

Blender

1 tbsp (15 mL) extra virgin olive oil

1 onion, chopped

1 clove garlic, chopped

½ red bell pepper, finely chopped

10 oz (300 g) frozen corn kernels, thawed

1½ cups (375 mL) cubed peeled yellow-fleshed potatoes

2 cups (500 mL) ready-to-use no-salt-added vegetable broth or Homemade Veggie Stock (page 59)

1 bay leaf

4 cups (1 L) unsweetened plain soy milk

1½ cups (375 mL) cooked quinoa (see page 51)

2 tsp (10 mL) dried dillweed

1 tsp (5 mL) salt

½ tsp (2 mL) freshly ground black pepper

1. In a large pot, heat oil over medium-high heat. Add onion and cook, stirring, for about 5 minutes or until translucent. Add garlic, red pepper, corn and potatoes; cook, stirring, until heated through.
2. Stir in broth and bay leaf; bring to a boil. Reduce heat and simmer for 10 minutes. Discard bay leaf.
3. Scoop 2 cups (500 mL) of the soup into the blender, add milk and purée until smooth.
4. Return purée to the soup and stir in quinoa, dill, salt and pepper; bring to a simmer. Simmer for 2 minutes or until heated through.

tips

Frozen corn often comes in 10-oz (300 g) packages. If you buy a larger bag, simply measure about 2 cups (500 mL).

If you'd like to prepare this chowder in advance, let it cool completely, then transfer to airtight containers and store in the refrigerator for up to 4 days.

CURRIED CHICKPEAS AND KALE

FOR TASTY PLANT-BASED food, look to a cuisine that has been making an art form of it for centuries. The spices and flavors of Indian vegetarian food make it one of the most beloved meatless options out there. This quick curry is a delicious example of the Indian way with beans. Serve it over hot cooked quinoa (see page 51), with roasted broccoli and onion (see page 47) on the side.

MAKES 4 SERVINGS

1 tbsp (15 mL) canola oil

1 onion, chopped

1 tbsp (15 mL) ground cumin

1 tbsp (15 mL) ground coriander

½ tsp (2 mL) ground turmeric

¼ tsp (1 mL) cayenne pepper

14-oz (398 mL) can diced tomatoes, with juice

2 cups (500 mL) packed chopped kale (tough stems and center ribs removed)

½ tsp (2 mL) salt

1½ cups (375 mL) cooked chickpeas (see page 55)

¼ cup (60 mL) packed fresh cilantro leaves, coarsely chopped

1 tbsp (15 mL) freshly squeezed lemon juice

½ cup (125 mL) roasted cashews

1. In a large skillet, heat oil over medium-high heat. Add onion and cook, stirring, until sizzling. Reduce heat to medium and cook, stirring, for 5 minutes or until tender. Add cumin, coriander, turmeric and cayenne; cook, stirring, for 1 minute.
2. Stir in tomatoes, kale and salt; cook, stirring occasionally, for 1 minute or until kale is wilted. Add chickpeas, stirring well. Reduce heat, cover and simmer for about 5 minutes, stirring occasionally, until thick. Remove from heat and stir in cilantro and lemon juice. Serve sprinkled with cashews.

tip

If you spill curry on a white countertop, be sure to wipe it up immediately or the counter will be stained by the turmeric.

variation

Try this with fresh mint instead of cilantro.

ROASTED CAULIFLOWER AND WALNUT BURRITOS
WITH CHERRY TOMATO SALSA

CAULIFLOWER AND WALNUTS combine for an almost beefy filling in this burrito, and "nooch" gives it a rich, cheesy quality. Smoky chipotle adds umami and a little heat. The salsa is so easy and quick, you can toss it together in a hurry.

MAKES 4 BURRITOS

ROASTED CAULIFLOWER AND WALNUT BURRITOS

5 cups (1.25 L) roasted cauliflower (see page 48), finely chopped

1 cup (250 mL) walnut halves, chopped

¼ cup (60 mL) nutritional yeast

½ tsp (2 mL) chipotle chile powder

½ tsp (2 mL) salt

Four 10-inch (25 cm) whole wheat tortillas

2 cups (500 mL) packed spinach leaves, chopped

CHERRY TOMATO SALSA

2 cups (500 mL) cherry tomatoes, chopped

½ cup (125 mL) packed fresh cilantro leaves, chopped

¼ cup (60 mL) minced shallots

½ tsp (2 mL) salt

½ tsp (2 mL) hot pepper sauce

1. **BURRITOS:** In a large bowl, combine cauliflower, walnuts, yeast, chile powder and salt. Set aside.

2. **SALSA:** In a medium bowl, combine tomatoes, cilantro, shallots, salt and hot pepper sauce.

3. Place tortillas on a work surface and place one-quarter of the cauliflower filling in the center of each. Pile spinach on top. Fold in ends, roll up tortillas and place one burrito, seam side down, on each serving plate. Serve with salsa.

tips

The combination of sweetly roasted cauliflower and rich, earthy walnuts has a meaty quality that will satisfy your savory cravings.

If making the burritos in advance, wrap each one in plastic wrap or waxed paper and refrigerate for up to 2 days.

variation

Tomato Cilantro Salsa (page 65) or Mango Sriracha Sauce (page 64) would be a nice switch for the cherry tomato salsa.

THAI RED CURRY EGGPLANT STEW
WITH TOFU AND BLACK RICE

THAI FOOD IS a vegan's friend. Creamy coconut milk combines with a riot of savory, spicy flavors in curry paste for an instantly exotic meal. Eggplant and peppers simmer to tender perfection as the tofu soaks up the creamy sauce, and a kick of lime zest brings it all together. Serve with Whole-Grain Biscuits (page 42).

MAKES 4 SERVINGS

12 oz (375 g) water-packed extra-firm tofu

14-oz (400 mL) can coconut milk, chilled for at least 1 hour or overnight

2 tbsp (30 mL) Thai red curry paste

2 cups (500 mL) cubed eggplant (about 8 oz/ 250 g)

1 red bell pepper, chopped

½ lime, zest pared in a long strip

2 tbsp (30 mL) packed brown sugar (or to taste)

¼ tsp (1 mL) salt

1 tbsp (15 mL) freshly squeezed lime juice

1 tbsp (15 mL) tamari

3 cups (750 mL) cooked black rice (see page 52), reheated

1 cup (250 mL) packed fresh basil leaves, coarsely chopped

1. Drain tofu and wrap in a clean tea towel, pressing gently to remove excess water. Cut into cubes and set aside.

2. Open can of coconut milk and scoop the thick cream on top into a large skillet. Bring to a boil over medium-high heat. Add curry paste, mashing to mix well, reduce heat and simmer, stirring occasionally, until fragrant.

3. Stir in the remaining coconut milk and return to a boil. Stir in eggplant, red pepper and lime zest; return to a boil. Reduce heat, cover, leaving the lid ajar, and simmer for about 8 minutes or until eggplant is tender. Stir in brown sugar, salt, lime juice and tamari. Taste and adjust curry paste or tamari as desired. Stir in tofu and simmer for 5 minutes. Discard lime zest.

4. Serve curry over rice, topped with basil.

tip

Paring the lime zest and simmering it in the sauce allows the oils from the zest to flavor the sauce without adding the chewiness of shredded zest.

variation

If you are not a fan of eggplant, you can substitute zucchini or even green beans and simmer just until tender-crisp.

CREAMY KALE SOUP
WITH ALMONDS

KALE IS THE nutrition superstar of greens, with protein, calcium, iron and traces of the omega-3 fats we need, so adding it to your menus is a good thing. In this soup, the leaves disappear into a creamy purée, so even kale avoiders will enjoy it. Creamy sweet potato, aromatic rosemary and crunchy toasted almonds add excitement and keep you coming back for another spoonful. Serve it with Pizza Bread (page 167).

MAKES 4 SERVINGS

Blender or food processor

1 tbsp (15 mL) olive oil

1 onion, chopped

1 lb (500 g) kale, tough stems and center ribs removed, chopped (about 6 cups/1.5 L)

1 cup (250 mL) mashed baked sweet potato (see page 45)

1 tbsp (15 mL) fresh rosemary leaves

1 cup (250 mL) ready-to-use vegetable broth or Homemade Veggie Stock (page 59)

2 cups (500 mL) unsweetened plain soy milk

½ tsp (2 mL) salt (approx.)

Freshly cracked black pepper

½ cup (125 mL) sliced almonds, toasted (see tip)

4 sprigs fresh rosemary

1. In a large pot, heat oil over medium-high heat. Add onion and cook, stirring, until sizzling. Reduce heat to medium and cook, stirring, for as long as you have time, at least 10 minutes, until onion is soft and golden, or up to 2 hours to caramelize it. Reduce the heat to medium-low if the onion starts to stick.

2. Stir in kale, sweet potato, rosemary and broth; bring to a boil over medium-high heat. Cover, reduce heat to low and simmer for about 10 minutes or until kale is tender. Remove from heat.

3. In batches as necessary, transfer soup to blender, add milk and purée until smooth. (Or transfer soup to food processor and purée until smooth, then add milk and process to blend.)

4. Return soup to the pot to reheat, if needed. Stir in salt and several grinds of pepper. Taste and adjust seasoning as desired. Serve topped with almonds and rosemary.

tip

Toast sliced almonds in a dry skillet over medium heat, stirring constantly, for 3 to 5 minutes or until golden and fragrant. Immediately transfer to a bowl to cool.

variation

Other leafy greens, like spinach or even cabbage, can stand in for kale. Use about 5 cups (1.25 L) chopped.

SPAGHETTI
WITH CAULIFLOWER AND CHICKPEAS

WHEN YOU WALK through the door after work, you'll be so glad you made that spaghetti sauce and roasted some cauliflower. This crowd-pleasing pasta comes together in minutes and delivers all the great Italian flavor we've come to love. Serve it with Everyday Green Salad (page 156) with Basil Vinaigrette (page 162).

MAKES 4 SERVINGS

8 oz (250 g) dried whole wheat spaghetti

3 cups (750 mL) roasted cauliflower (see page 48)

1 cup (250 mL) cooked chickpeas (see page 55)

1 cup (250 mL) Veggie Spaghetti Sauce (page 61)

2 tbsp (30 mL) chopped drained kalamata olives

Cashew Parmesan (page 69)

1. In a large pot of boiling salted water, cook spaghetti according to package directions until al dente, about 9 minutes. Drain well.
2. Return the pot to medium heat and add cauliflower, chickpeas and spaghetti sauce, stirring well. Return spaghetti to the pot and add olives; cook, stirring until heated through and the sauce coats the spaghetti. Serve hot, sprinkled with Cashew Parmesan.

tips

Green olives or 1 tbsp (15 mL) drained capers can be substituted for the kalamata olives.

Using the same pot to cook the spaghetti and heat the sauce means you don't need to wash two pots.

TEMPEH PASTA SALAD
WITH TOMATO AND AVOCADO

PASTA SALADS ARE usually goopy, mayonnaise-laden affairs, but not this one. The tender pasta is slicked with a tomato vinaigrette, and the chewy chunks of tempeh have a maple and smoked paprika flavor that really makes them sing. Add some chunks of creamy avocado, and you'll forget all about cheese.

MAKES 4 SERVINGS

4 oz (125 g) dried whole wheat rotini pasta

24 slices Baked Marinated Tempeh (page 57), cut into bite-size pieces

1 tomato, chopped

1 avocado, cubed

1 stalk celery, chopped

¼ cup (60 mL) packed fresh parsley leaves, chopped

2 tbsp (30 mL) chopped red onion

1 clove garlic, minced

1 tsp (5 mL) dried thyme

1 tsp (5 mL) salt

½ tsp (2 mL) freshly ground black pepper

1 tbsp (15 mL) balsamic vinegar

1 tsp (5 mL) tomato paste

2 tbsp (30 mL) extra virgin olive oil

1. In a large pot of boiling salted water, cook pasta according to package directions until al dente, about 11 minutes.
2. Meanwhile, in a large bowl, combine tempeh, tomato, avocado, celery, parsley and red onion.
3. In a cup, using a fork, stir together garlic, thyme, salt, pepper, vinegar and tomato paste. Stir in oil.
4. Drain pasta, rinse with cool water, and drain again. Add pasta to the tempeh mixture. Drizzle salad with dressing and toss to coat.

tips

Summertime is pasta salad season. Be sure to cook the pasta to al dente, so it will not get soggy as it sits.

If you want to prepare this salad in advance, omit the avocado. Cover the salad tightly and refrigerate for up to 2 days. Add the avocado and toss to combine just before serving.

variation

When fresh herbs are plentiful, try replacing the parsley with fresh basil, arugula or dillweed.

SWEET POTATO SOUP
WITH SPINACH

BAKING SWEET POTATOES makes them even sweeter and more intense, and when you purée them for this soup, you'll be amazed by how rich and decadent it tastes. Stirring in spinach at the end gives it some color and texture, and a dash of vinegar cuts the sweetness just enough to wake up your taste buds. Serve the soup with Whole-Grain Biscuits (page 42) and Tomato Basil Salad (page 159).

MAKES 4 SERVINGS

1 tbsp (15 mL) extra virgin olive oil

1 onion, chopped

3 cups (750 mL) mashed baked sweet potato (see page 45)

2 cups (500 mL) ready-to-use vegetable broth or Homemade Veggie Stock (page 59)

¼ cup (60 mL) nutritional yeast

1 tsp (5 mL) dried thyme

½ tsp (2 mL) salt

1 cup (250 mL) unsweetened plain soy milk

4 cups (1 L) packed spinach leaves

½ cup (125 mL) packed fresh parsley leaves, chopped

1 tsp (5 mL) apple cider vinegar

½ cup (125 mL) chopped walnuts

1. In a large pot, heat oil over medium-high heat. Add onion and cook, stirring, until sizzling. Reduce heat to medium and cook, stirring, for as long as you have time, at least 10 minutes, until onion is soft and golden, or up to 2 hours to caramelize it. Reduce the heat to medium-low if the onion starts to stick.

2. Add sweet potato and broth, whisking until well blended. Stir in yeast, thyme, salt and milk; cook, stirring often, until starting to bubble around the edges.

3. Add spinach and parsley; cook, stirring, until spinach is just wilted. If the soup seems too thick, stir in a little more broth or milk. Stir in vinegar. Taste and adjust seasoning with thyme, salt and vinegar as desired. Serve immediately, sprinkled with walnuts.

tips

There are many colors of sweet potato, from white to shades of orange to purple. All of them would be delicious in this soup. You'll need about 2 lbs (1 kg) of sweet potatoes to make 3 cups (750 mL) mashed.

Soy milk offers the most protein of all the nondairy options, but any nondairy milk can be substituted in this recipe.

variation

For a richer soup, try using an unsweetened nondairy creamer in place of the soy milk.

ROASTED CARROT SOUP
WITH BARLEY AND PESTO

ROASTING CARROTS ON the weekend is so easy. You don't even have to cut them up — just throw them in the oven whole. Then you'll be set for this lovely soup, studded with chewy barley and garnished with herby pesto and crunchy almonds. Serve with Sweet Potato Cornbread (page 43).

MAKES 4 SERVINGS

Blender

1 tbsp (15 mL) extra virgin olive oil

1 onion, chopped

1 lb 10 oz (800 g) roasted carrots (see page 47), sliced

1 cup (250 mL) ready-to-use vegetable broth or Homemade Veggie Stock (page 59)

1 cup (250 mL) unsweetened plain soy milk

½ tsp (2 mL) salt

1 cup (250 mL) cooked barley (see page 49)

¼ cup (60 mL) nutritional yeast

¼ cup (60 mL) Basil Pesto (page 66)

½ cup (125 mL) slivered almonds

1. In a large skillet, heat oil over medium-high heat. Add onion and cook, stirring, until sizzling. Reduce heat to medium and cook, stirring, for as long as you have time, at least 10 minutes, until onion is soft and golden, or up to 2 hours to caramelize it. Reduce the heat to medium-low if the onion starts to stick.

2. Place carrots in blender. Scrape in onion and oil, then add broth, milk and salt. Blend until smooth, scraping down the sides of the container as needed.

3. Scrape purée into a large pot, add barley and yeast; cook, stirring, over medium heat until heated through.

4. Divide soup among bowls and swirl 1 tbsp (15 mL) pesto on top of each. Sprinkle with almonds.

tips

Roasting vegetables makes them shrink and become more concentrated, so you'll need to roast about 2½ lbs (1.25 kg) carrots to get the amount needed for this recipe. After slicing the roasted carrots, you should have about 5 cups (1.25 L).

This soup is thick and creamy by design, but you can always make it a little thinner by adding more soy milk or broth.

If you like to serve toast with your soup, you can leave out the barley.

TOFU QUINOA BURGERS

WHY DO WE love burgers so much? Veggie burgers are the perfect vehicle for quinoa and tofu, with crispy edges and savory centers to bite into. Once you have them prepped, they are a meal in themselves, with an Asian Cucumber Salad (page 158) on the side, or they make a great topping for a grain bowl at lunch (see page 114).

MAKES 8 BURGERS | Preheat oven to 400°F (200°C)

Blender

Rimmed baking sheet, lined with parchment paper

¼ cup (60 mL) large-flake (old-fashioned) rolled oats

1 cup (250 mL) cooked quinoa (see page 51)

1 tsp (5 mL) extra virgin olive oil

¼ cup (60 mL) minced carrot

¼ cup (60 mL) minced green onion

¼ cup (60 mL) packed fresh parsley leaves, chopped

1 lb (500 g) water-packed extra-firm tofu

1 tsp (5 mL) dried thyme or sage

1 tsp (5 mL) paprika

¾ tsp (3 mL) salt

¼ cup (60 mL) almond butter

1 tsp (5 mL) tamari

4 whole wheat hamburger buns

1. Place oats in blender and grind to a coarse flour.
2. Pour oat flour into a large bowl and stir in quinoa; set aside.
3. In a small skillet, heat oil over medium heat. Add carrot and green onion; cook, stirring, for 3 to 4 minutes or until carrot is soft. Stir in parsley and cook, stirring, until slightly wilted. Add carrot mixture to the quinoa mixture.

4. Drain tofu and wrap in a clean tea towel, pressing gently to remove excess water. Crumble tofu into the quinoa mixture. Add thyme, paprika, salt, almond butter and tamari, kneading with your hands until the mixture is well combined and holds its shape when pressed.
5. Measure rounded, packed ¼-cup (60 mL) portions and place them at least 1 inch (2.5 cm) apart on prepared baking sheet. Press each with the palm of your hand to flatten it to ½ inch (1 cm) thick.
6. Bake in preheated oven for 20 minutes or until tops are brown and a nice crust has formed.
7. Serve 4 burgers hot, on hamburger buns. Let the other 4 cool completely on a wire rack, then store in an airtight container in the refrigerator for up to 4 days.

tips

If you have oat flour on hand, you can use it in place of the large-flake oats and skip step 1.

Water-packed extra-firm tofu has a spongy texture that works well in burgers.

You'll need a full pound (500 g) of tofu for these burgers. If you can only find packages in other sizes, cube and freeze the leftovers to use in stir-fries. Frozen tofu, once thawed, absorbs flavor and has a chewy texture you'll love.

BIG NUTTY CAESAR SALAD

THE TYPICAL CAESAR contains anchovies and Parmesan cheese, and has a creamy, egg-based dressing. In this delicious version, a creamy cashew dressing spiked with olives gives you all the same bang for the buck. Serve with Lemony Pesto Beets (page 166).

MAKES 4 SERVINGS

½ cup (125 mL) Creamy Cashew Dressing (page 164)

2 tsp (10 mL) black olive paste (vegan tapenade)

4 slices whole wheat bread

5 oz (150 g) baby romaine lettuce

½ cup (125 mL) slivered almonds, toasted (see tip, page 142)

1. Measure cashew dressing and stir in olive paste; set aside.
2. Toast the bread on a darker setting, then cut into 1-inch (2.5 cm) croutons. Let cool.
3. Place romaine in a large bowl, drizzle with dressing and toss to coat.
4. Divide salad among four serving plates or bowls and top with croutons and almonds. Serve immediately.

tips

Black olive paste is a concentrated source of umami and flavor. Once you buy a jar, you'll want to spread it on sandwiches, stir it into pastas and dollop it in soups.

Of course you can use purchased croutons, or gluten-free ones.

to pack for lunch

If you're making this salad to pack for lunch instead, pack romaine and dressing in separate food storage containers. Refrigerate for up to 2 days. Pack the croutons and almonds together in sandwich-size sealable plastic bags.

PESTO PASTA
WITH BROCCOLI AND CARROTS

YOUR PREPPED PESTO is waiting for you, ready to make this classic pasta for a
busy weeknight. Adding broccoli and carrots to the pot of pasta right at the end gives
you some veggies without having to use another pot, making it even quicker. Serve with a
Green Salad with Cashew Dressing (page 157).

MAKES 4 SERVINGS

8 oz (250 g) dried whole wheat rotini pasta

1 large carrot, julienned (see tip)

3 cups (750 mL) bite-size broccoli florets (about
8 oz/250 g)

½ cup (125 mL) Basil Pesto (page 66)

½ cup (125 mL) grape tomatoes, halved

½ cup (125 mL) Cashew Parmesan (page 69)

1. In a large pot of boiling salted water, cook
   pasta according to package directions until
   al dente, about 11 minutes, adding carrot
   and broccoli about 1 minute before the end
   of the cooking time. Drain well, shaking
   the colander.
2. Return pasta mixture to the pot, add pesto
   and toss to coat. If desired, warm over
   medium heat. Add tomatoes, toss and
   serve sprinkled with Cashew Parmesan.

tips

To julienne the carrot, use a chef's knife to
thinly slice it on a diagonal. Stack the slices
and cut them into ¼-inch (0.5 cm) slivers.

Cooking the vegetables by adding them to
the boiling pasta is an easy way to save
time. If you prefer your vegetables a little
softer, add them to the pot sooner.

If you want to prepare this dish in advance,
cover it tightly and refrigerate for up to
4 days. It's delicious cold or reheated.

variation

Substitute cauliflower for broccoli, or
add some chopped red bell pepper for
some variety.

"MAC AND CHEESE"
WITH A NUTTY CRUNCH TOPPING

WE ALL LOVE macaroni and cheese, and your search for a great recipe that will meet your cravings is over. Making the Creamy Cheesy Sauce on prep day sets up a few cheesy meals, and this is the peak of the week! Edamame and almonds give you plant-based protein. Serve this with Crispy Kale with Lemon (page 165).

MAKES 4 SERVINGS | Preheat oven to 400°F (200°C)

8-inch (20 cm) square baking pan, lightly oiled

8 oz (250 g) dried whole wheat macaroni

½ cup (125 mL) frozen shelled edamame, thawed

1½ cups (375 mL) Creamy Cheesy Sauce (page 62)

¼ cup (60 mL) panko

2 tbsp (30 mL) slivered almonds, toasted (see tip)

½ tsp (2 mL) extra virgin olive oil

1. In a large pot of boiling salted water, cook macaroni according to package directions until al dente, about 7 minutes. Drain well.
2. Return macaroni to the pot and stir in edamame and sauce. Spread in prepared baking pan.
3. In a medium bowl, combine panko, almonds and oil. Sprinkle over macaroni mixture.
4. Bake in preheated oven for 20 minutes or until crumbs are toasted and macaroni is bubbling around the edges. Serve immediately.

tips

Toast slivered almonds in a dry skillet over medium heat, stirring constantly, for 3 to 5 minutes or until golden and fragrant. Immediately transfer to a bowl to cool.

Store any leftovers, tightly covered, in the refrigerator for up to 4 days.

CREAMY SQUASH SOUP
WITH FARRO AND SAGE

ROASTED SQUASH IS a great soup waiting to happen, packed with hearty orange sweetness. Sage is often paired with squash because the two make beautiful music together. Cooked farro gives it some texture and hefty whole-grain goodness. Serve with hot Whole-Grain Biscuits (page 42).

MAKES 4 SERVINGS

Blender

1½ tbsp (22 mL) canola oil

3 onions, chopped

3 cups (750 mL) mashed roasted squash (see page 48)

3 cups (750 mL) unsweetened plain soy milk

1 tsp (5 mL) salt

1½ tbsp (22 mL) dried sage

1½ cups (375 mL) cooked farro or wheat berries (see page 50)

1. In a large pot, heat oil over medium-high heat. Add onions and cook, stirring, until sizzling. Reduce heat to medium-low and cook, stirring, for about 10 minutes or until soft and golden.
2. Meanwhile, in blender, combine squash, milk and salt; purée until smooth (see tip).
3. Add sage to the onions and cook, stirring, for 1 minute or until fragrant. Stir in squash purée. Stir in farro and cook until heated through. Serve hot.

tips

Because squash varies in moisture content, you may need a little more soy milk.

Soy milk offers the most protein of all the nondairy options, but any nondairy milk can be substituted in this recipe.

variation

Instead of sage, try 2 tsp (10 mL) curry powder or 1 tbsp (15 mL) dried thyme.

BLACK BEAN AND SWEET POTATO CURRY

FORGET BORING MEALS once you have curry recipes in your back pocket. In this black bean curry, you get subtle spicing and a balance of sweet and sour, all in a smooth purée. It's comfort food for grown-ups. Serve with whole wheat flatbreads and Broccolini with Peanuts (page 166).

MAKES 4 SERVINGS

Blender

2 tsp (10 mL) canola oil

1 onion, chopped

1 red bell pepper, chopped

1 tbsp (15 mL) chopped gingerroot

2 tsp (10 mL) ground cumin

1/2 tsp (2 mL) ground turmeric

1/4 tsp (1 mL) cayenne pepper

1 cup (250 mL) coarsely mashed baked sweet potato (see page 45)

1 cup (250 mL) cooked black beans (see page 54)

1/2 tsp (2 mL) salt

2 cups (500 mL) ready-to-use vegetable broth or Homemade Veggie Stock (page 59)

1/2 cup (125 mL) packed fresh cilantro leaves

1. In a large skillet, heat oil over medium-high heat. Add onion and cook, stirring, until sizzling. Reduce heat to medium and cook, stirring, for about 5 minutes or until translucent. Add red pepper, ginger, cumin, turmeric and cayenne; cook, stirring, for about 3 minutes or until pepper is softened.
2. In blender, combine sweet potato, beans, salt and broth; purée until smooth.
3. Add purée to onion mixture and stir to combine; bring to a simmer. Simmer, stirring often, for 5 minutes, adding a little water if it gets too thick. Serve sprinkled with cilantro.

tip

Sautéing the spices with the onion deepens their flavor without the risk of burning or over-toasting.

variation

Roasted squash (see page 48) or carrots (see page 47) could stand in for the sweet potato.

SPAGHETTI
WITH BROCCOLINI AND CHERRY TOMATOES

ROAST BROCCOLINI UNTIL it has a little char on the edges, for a hint of bitterness and complexity, and then the classic combination of spaghetti, good olive oil and lemon will teach you why Italians like to keep their pasta simple. Serve with Garlic Toast and a Green Salad with Cashew Dressing (page 157) on the side.

MAKES 4 SERVINGS

8 oz (250 g) dried whole wheat spaghetti

2 tbsp (30 mL) extra virgin olive oil

2 cloves garlic, chopped

1 tsp (5 mL) grated lemon zest

½ tsp (2 mL) hot pepper flakes (or to taste)

3 cups (750 mL) roasted broccolini (see page 47)

1 cup (250 mL) cherry tomatoes, halved

½ tsp (2 mL) salt

½ cup (125 mL) Cashew Parmesan (page 69)

1. In a large pot of boiling salted water, cook spaghetti according to package directions until al dente, about 9 minutes. Drain well.
2. Meanwhile, in a large skillet, heat oil over medium-high heat. Add garlic and stir for a few seconds, then add lemon zest and hot pepper flakes, stirring just until sizzling. Add broccolini, tomatoes and salt; cook, stirring, for about 4 minutes or until tomatoes are starting to shrivel and shrink.
3. Add spaghetti to the skillet and toss with tongs to mix; cook until warmed through. Serve immediately, sprinkled with Cashew Parmesan.

GARLIC TOAST

Preheat oven to 350°F (180°C). Cut two 6-inch (15 cm) baguette pieces into ½-inch (1 cm) slices, place on a baking sheet and brush with olive oil. Sprinkle with Cashew Parmesan (made with the optional garlic). Bake for about 10 minutes or until crisp. Serve hot.

BLACK BEAN AND SQUASH CHILI
WITH DUMPLINGS

YOU COULD JUST make the chili and skip the dumplings, but why would you when you get a delicious layer of mini whole-grain biscuits floating on a hearty stew of beans and veggies? With your homemade baking mix prepped and ready, dumplings are a snap.

MAKES 4 SERVINGS | Preheat oven to 400°F (200°C)

8-cup (2 L) shallow baking dish

BLACK BEAN AND SQUASH CHILI

1 tbsp (15 mL) olive oil

1 onion, chopped

2 cloves garlic, chopped

1 carrot, chopped

1 red bell pepper, chopped

1 tbsp (15 mL) ground cumin

1 tbsp (15 mL) chili powder

1 tsp (5 mL) chipotle chile powder

¼ tsp (1 mL) ground cinnamon

2 cups (500 mL) water

1 cup (250 mL) coarsely mashed roasted squash (see page 48)

¼ cup (60 mL) tomato paste

1 tsp (5 mL) salt

1½ cups (375 mL) cooked black beans (see page 54)

¼ cup (60 mL) nutritional yeast

1 tsp (5 mL) dried oregano

¼ cup (60 mL) chopped fresh cilantro

DUMPLINGS

1½ cups (375 mL) Whole-Grain Baking Mix (page 41)

½ cup + 1 tbsp (140 mL) unsweetened plain soy milk

1 tbsp (15 mL) apple cider vinegar

1 green onion, chopped

1. **CHILI:** In a large, heavy pot, heat oil over medium-high heat. Add onion and cook, stirring, until sizzling. Reduce heat to medium and cook, stirring, for 5 minutes or until softened. Add garlic, carrot and red pepper; cook, stirring, for 5 minutes or until carrot is tender. Stir in cumin, chili powder, chipotle chile powder and cinnamon; cook, stirring, for 1 minute.

2. In a large bowl, whisk together water, squash, tomato paste and salt. Add to the pot, increase heat and bring to a boil. Add beans, yeast and oregano; bring to a simmer. Reduce heat and simmer, stirring occasionally, for about 5 minutes or until slightly thickened. Transfer to baking dish and stir in cilantro.

3. **DUMPLINGS:** Place baking mix in a large bowl. In a cup, combine milk and vinegar; let stand for 1 minute to curdle, then pour over baking mix. Sprinkle in green onion and stir just until flour is all moistened.

4. Scoop up rounded tablespoons (15 mL) of dough and drop them on the chili in the baking dish, spacing them evenly.

5. Bake in preheated oven for 25 minutes or until chili is bubbling up around the edges and dumplings are golden brown. Serve hot.

tips

This works best when the chili is hot, but not boiling, at the time that you add the dumplings. If your chili has cooled, the dumplings may not bake through to the bottom.

Save any leftovers in a tightly covered container for up to 4 days.

variation

Add ¼ cup (60 mL) chopped roasted red peppers to the dumpling dough instead of green onions.

THAI YELLOW CURRY
TOFU WITH NOODLES

THIS CREAMY, GOLDEN curry is luscious, especially when you sear some meaty shiitakes to sprinkle on top. Serve with Everyday Green Salad (page 156) with Sesame-Miso Garlic Dressing (page 163).

MAKES 4 SERVINGS

12 oz (375 g) water-packed extra-firm tofu

1 cup (250 mL) coconut milk

½ tsp (2 mL) ground turmeric

1 tbsp (15 mL) Thai yellow curry paste

1 lime, zest pared in a long strip

½ tsp (2 mL) salt

1 cup (250 mL) ready-to-use vegetable broth or Homemade Veggie Stock (page 59)

1 jalapeño pepper, seeded and chopped

2 cups (500 mL) cubed sweet potatoes

8 oz (250 g) flat rice noodles

1 tsp (5 mL) canola or coconut oil

4 oz (125 g) shiitake mushrooms, stems removed, caps slivered

Fresh cilantro leaves

Chopped green onion

1. Drain tofu and wrap in a clean tea towel, pressing gently to remove excess water. Cut into cubes and set aside.
2. In a large skillet, bring coconut milk, turmeric and curry paste to a boil over medium-high heat, stirring. Stir in lime zest, salt and broth; bring to a simmer. Reduce heat and simmer for 5 minutes, adding water or more broth if it gets too thick.
3. Stir in jalapeño and sweet potatoes; increase heat and bring to a boil. Reduce heat to low, cover and simmer for about 8 minutes or until sweet potatoes are tender when pierced with a knife. Fold in tofu and simmer gently, uncovered, stirring occasionally, for about 4 minutes or until sauce is thick.
4. Meanwhile, in a large pot of boiling salted water, cook noodles according to package directions, about 4 minutes.
5. In another skillet, heat oil over high heat. Add slivered mushrooms and cook, stirring, for about 2 minutes or until browned and shrunken. Keep warm.
6. Drain noodles and divide among four plates. Ladle curry over noodles and top with mushrooms, cilantro and green onion.

tip

Searing the shiitakes makes them chewy and meaty, and serving them on top gives you some visual and textural contrast.

variation

In summertime, substitute a mix of green beans and carrots for the sweet potatoes.

MUMBAI LENTILS AND KALE

QUICK-COOKING RED LENTILS combine with kale for a delicious mix of colors and textures. Pick up whole wheat flatbreads to dip in the warm, chunky curry, and you'll be in heaven. This is a big batch — you'll be saving almost half of it for lunches later in the week.

MAKES 4 SERVINGS, PLUS LEFTOVERS FOR LUNCH

4 tsp (20 mL) canola oil

1 tbsp (15 mL) black mustard seeds

1 tbsp (15 mL) cumin seeds

2 onions, chopped

2 carrots, chopped

2 jalapeño peppers, seeded and minced

1 cup (250 mL) dried red lentils

2 tbsp (30 mL) chopped gingerroot

½ tsp (2 mL) ground turmeric

4 cups (1 L) ready-to-use vegetable broth or Homemade Veggie Stock (page 59)

2 lbs (1 kg) kale, tough stems and center ribs removed, leaves chopped (about 12 cups/3 L)

1 tsp (5 mL) salt

14-oz (398 mL) can tomato purée

¼ cup (60 mL) freshly squeezed lemon juice

4 whole wheat flatbreads, warmed

1. In a large skillet, heat oil over medium-high heat. Add mustard and cumin seeds; cook, stirring, for about 30 seconds or until fragrant and the mustard seeds start to pop and turn gray. Add onions and cook, stirring, for about 5 minutes or until translucent.

2. Stir in carrots, jalapeños, lentils, ginger, turmeric and broth; bring to a boil. Reduce heat to medium-low, cover and simmer, stirring occasionally, for about 25 minutes or until lentils are tender.

3. Stir in kale, salt, tomato purée and lemon juice; simmer, uncovered, stirring often, for 5 to 10 minutes or until kale is softened to your liking and dark green. Serve hot, with warm flatbreads.

tips

Before serving, set aside the 3 cups (750 mL) you'll need for Sweet Potato and Mumbai Lentils (page 123) in a food storage container. Let cool completely before covering and refrigerating.

Serve with roasted broccoli (see page 46) on the side.

TEMPEH MEATLOAF

MEATLOAF IS HOME-STYLE comfort food, something most of us grew up with. The chunky texture of tempeh creates a meaty, hearty loaf laced with herbs and veggies. Brown rice gives it a meat-like chew, and whole wheat bread crumbs bind it for a sliceable loaf. Save half for your meatloaf sandwiches later in the week. Serve with roasted carrots (see page 47) and Everyday Green Salad (page 156) with Balsamic Vinaigrette (page 161).

MAKES 8 SERVINGS | Preheat oven to 350°F (180°C)

8- by 4-inch (20 by 10 cm) metal loaf pan

2 tbsp (30 mL) extra virgin olive oil

2 stalks celery, chopped

1 onion, chopped

1 carrot, minced

4 cloves garlic, minced

1 lb (500 g) tempeh, minced and crumbled

½ cup (125 mL) ready-to-use vegetable broth or Homemade Veggie Stock (page 59)

¼ cup (60 mL) white miso

2 tbsp (30 mL) tamari

1 tbsp (15 mL) dried sage

1 cup (250 mL) cooked medium-grain brown rice (see page 53)

¾ cup (175 mL) fresh whole wheat bread crumbs

½ cup (125 mL) packed fresh parsley leaves, chopped

¼ cup (60 mL) ground flax seeds (flaxseed meal)

1. In a large skillet, heat oil over medium-high heat. Add celery, onion and carrot; cook, stirring, for about 5 minutes or until onion is soft and translucent. Add garlic and cook, stirring, for 1 minute. Add tempeh and cook briefly, breaking it up with your spatula.

2. In a cup, whisk together broth, miso and tamari. Add broth mixture and sage to the pan and bring to a boil, stirring often. Boil, stirring and scraping the pan often, for about 5 minutes or until all the liquid has evaporated.

3. Scrape tempeh mixture into a large bowl and add rice, bread crumbs, parsley and flax seeds, mashing and mixing well. Let stand until cool enough to touch, then knead with your hands, crushing the tempeh. Press tempeh mixture firmly into loaf pan and cover with foil.

4. Bake in preheated oven for 45 minutes. Uncover and bake for 25 minutes or until crusty on top. Let cool on a wire rack for at least 5 minutes before serving (see tip).

tips

Before serving, cut the loaf in half. Cut one half into 4 slices and serve hot. Let the other half cool completely on the rack, then store in an airtight container to make Meatloaf Sandwiches (page 125) for lunch later in the week.

You can freeze slices of meatloaf, tightly wrapped, for up to 1 month. To reheat, thaw in the refrigerator overnight, then microwave each slice on High for about 1 minute.

SUSHI BOWLS
WITH AVOCADO, EDAMAME, PICKLED GINGER AND CABBAGE

THE POPULARITY OF bowls undoubtedly comes from the comforting ease of both making them and eating them — you can compose a pretty meal on top of the brown rice in just a few seconds. If you like sushi, you'll love the irresistible flavors of this bowl. For a Japanese-themed meal, serve with Quick Miso Soup (page 60).

MAKES 4 SERVINGS

4 cups (1 L) cooked medium-grain brown rice (see page 53)

1 tsp (5 mL) granulated sugar

2 tsp (10 mL) unseasoned rice vinegar

4 tsp (20 mL) wasabi paste (optional)

¼ cup (60 mL) vegan mayonnaise, such as Aquafaba Mayo (page 68)

2 avocados, sliced

8 oz (250 g) snow peas, trimmed

2 cups (500 mL) frozen shelled edamame, thawed

2 cups (500 mL) sliced red cabbage

¼ cup (60 mL) drained pickled ginger slices

Tamari

1. Place rice in a large bowl. In a small cup, stir together sugar and vinegar until sugar is dissolved, then drizzle over rice, folding it in gently so the rice stays separate. Portion rice into four shallow bowls.
2. If using wasabi, stir it into the mayo.
3. Arrange avocados, snow peas, edamame and cabbage on top of the rice in each bowl, dividing evenly. Arrange pickled ginger in the center and drizzle it all with mayo. Serve with tamari at the table.

tips

If you prefer, you can reheat the rice (see tip, page 53) before building the bowls.

Make extra wasabi mayo to use as a sandwich spread.

variation

Substitute leafy greens like kale or spinach for the cabbage, or add some kimchi for a spicy, funky accent.

JAMAICAN CURRIED BEANS AND GREENS

JAMAICA HAS ITS curries too, based on the plentiful coconut and spices that grow on the island. There's even a vegan cuisine in Jamaica, called Ital food, that is cooked and served by Rastafarians. Serve this vegan curry over medium-grain brown rice (see page 53), with Tropical Fruit Salad with Mint (page 160) on the side.

MAKES 4 SERVINGS

¾ cup (175 mL) coconut milk

½ cup (125 mL) ready-to-use vegetable broth or Homemade Veggie Stock (page 59)

4 green onions, white and green parts separated, cut into slivers

2 jalapeño peppers, seeded and chopped

2 cloves garlic, minced

1 tsp (5 mL) dried thyme

½ tsp (2 mL) ground turmeric

½ tsp (2 mL) ground allspice

½ tsp (2 mL) salt (approx.)

1 lb (500 g) kale, tough stems and center ribs removed, leaves cut into 1-inch (2.5 cm) pieces (about 6 cups/1.5 L)

1 red bell pepper, chopped

14-oz (398 mL) can red kidney beans (see tips), drained

Cayenne pepper or hot pepper sauce (optional)

1. Pour coconut milk and broth into a large skillet. Add white parts of green onions, jalapeños, garlic, thyme, turmeric, allspice and salt. Bring to a boil over medium-high heat, then reduce heat and simmer vigorously, stirring often, for about 2 minutes or until slightly thickened.

2. Stir in kale and red pepper; bring to a boil. Reduce heat and simmer, stirring occasionally, for about 5 minutes or until kale is your desired tenderness. Stir in beans and green parts of green onions; simmer until heated through. Taste and adjust seasoning with more salt or, if it is not hot enough, cayenne or hot pepper sauce to taste.

tips

If you happen to have cooked red kidney beans in the fridge or freezer, feel free to use them instead of canned. You'll need about 1½ cups (375 mL) for this recipe.

If you can only find larger can sizes, measure out 1½ cups (375 mL) beans to use in this recipe and store the rest in an airtight container in the refrigerator for up to 1 week.

MOROCCAN CHICKPEAS
OVER COUSCOUS WITH ROASTED BROCCOLI

COUSCOUS IS NEARLY an instant meal — all it takes is a few minutes to absorb boiling water or broth, and it is ready to make a warm, savory bed for Moroccan-spiced chickpeas, perfect for fast weeknight meals.

MAKES 4 SERVINGS

COUSCOUS WITH ROASTED BROCCOLI

1½ tsp (7 mL) olive oil

1 onion, chopped

2 cloves garlic, minced

1 tsp (5 mL) paprika

½ tsp (2 mL) freshly ground black pepper

1¼ cups (300 mL) water

½ tsp (2 mL) salt

1 cup (250 mL) whole wheat couscous

2 cups (500 mL) roasted broccoli (see page 46)

MOROCCAN CHICKPEAS

1½ tsp (7 mL) olive oil

1 tomato, chopped

14-oz (398 mL) can chickpeas (see tips), drained and rinsed

¼ cup (60 mL) raisins

1 tsp (5 mL) dried thyme

1 tsp (5 mL) ground cumin

½ tsp (2 mL) ground turmeric

½ tsp (2 mL) salt

1 cup (250 mL) slivered almonds, toasted (see tip, page 142)

1. **COUSCOUS:** In a medium saucepan, heat oil over medium heat. Add onion and cook, stirring, for about 5 minutes or until softened. Add garlic, paprika and pepper; cook, stirring, for 2 minutes.

2. Stir in water and salt; increase heat and bring to a boil. Remove from heat, sprinkle in couscous and stir once, then cover and let stand for 5 minutes. Quickly stir in broccoli, cover and let stand while you prepare the chickpeas.

3. **CHICKPEAS:** In a small saucepan, heat oil over medium-high heat. Add tomato and bring to a sizzle. Add chickpeas, raisins, thyme, cumin, turmeric and salt; cook, stirring, until chickpeas are coated and heated through.

4. Divide couscous evenly among serving plates, ladle chickpea mixture over top and sprinkle with almonds.

tips

If you happen to have cooked chickpeas in the fridge or freezer, feel free to use them instead of canned. You'll need about 1½ cups (375 mL) for this recipe.

If you can only find larger can sizes, measure out 1½ cups (375 mL) chickpeas to use in this recipe and store the rest in an airtight container in the refrigerator for up to 1 week.

SALADS, DRESSINGS AND SIDES

EVERYDAY GREEN SALAD

PREWASHED SALAD GREENS are such time-savers, but it's still a good idea to give them a rinse and spin them dry.

MAKES 4 SERVINGS

4 to 5 oz (125 to 150 g) salad greens (or 1 small head romaine lettuce)

1 small cucumber or tomato, chopped

1 handful sprouts or pea shoots

½ cup (125 mL) salad dressing

1. In a large bowl, combine greens, cucumber and sprouts. Drizzle with dressing and toss to coat. Serve immediately.

tip

Prewashed salad greens come in many varieties. Go with what appeals to you, from a hearty, deep green mix to a lighter, sweeter option.

variation

Chopped apples, orange segments or a handful of nuts make great salad toppers.

to pack for lunch

Divide undressed salad among four 3-cup (750 mL) food storage containers. Pack 2 tbsp (30 mL) dressing separately in each of four small containers. Refrigerate for up to 1 day.

GREEN SALAD
WITH CASHEW DRESSING

THE ONLY RULE when making salads is to pair a heavier creamy dressing with greens that can hold up to the weight. Crisp, sturdy greens like baby kale mixes or chopped romaine are perfect with a creamy cashew dressing.

MAKES 4 SERVINGS

4 oz (125 g) baby kale mix or other salad greens

½ cup (125 mL) Creamy Cashew Dressing (page 164)

1 small cucumber, peeled (if desired) and chopped

1. Place kale mix in a large bowl and drizzle with dressing, tossing to coat. Serve topped with cucumbers.

tip

Always wait to dress salads just before serving.

variations

GREEN SALAD WITH BALSAMIC VINAIGRETTE: Replace the cashew dressing with Balsamic Vinaigrette (page 161).

Any vegetables you have left over from the week, such as broccoli, cauliflower, bell peppers or cabbage, can stand in for the cucumber.

to pack for lunch

Divide kale mix and cucumber slices among four 1½- to 2-cup (375 to 500 mL) food storage containers. Pack 2 tbsp (30 mL) dressing separately in each of four small airtight containers. Refrigerate for up to 1 day.

ARUGULA SALAD

SHAKE UP YOUR salad routine with arugula. It goes well with Sesame-Miso Garlic Dressing (page 163), Balsamic Vinaigrette (page 161) and Basil Vinaigrette (page 162).

MAKES 4 SERVINGS

4 oz (125 g) baby arugula

1 tomato, cut into wedges

1 cup (250 mL) shredded carrot

½ cup (125 mL) salad dressing

tip

For 1 cup (250 mL) shredded carrot, you will need 1 large carrot. Shred it using a box grater or other grater.

1. In a large bowl, combine arugula, tomato and carrot. Drizzle with dressing and toss to coat. Serve immediately.

to pack for lunch

Divide undressed salad among four 3-cup (750 mL) food storage containers. Pack 2 tbsp (30 mL) dressing separately in each of four small airtight containers. Refrigerate for up to 1 day.

ASIAN CUCUMBER SALAD

COOL CUCUMBERS MAKE a perfect companion to your Asian meals, providing a refreshing, tangy bite in between bites of savory stir-fry or curry.

MAKES 4 SERVINGS

4 small cucumbers (about 1 lb/500 g total), peeled (if desired) and sliced

2 green onions, slivered

2 tbsp (30 mL) granulated sugar

½ tsp (2 mL) salt

¼ cup (60 mL) unseasoned rice vinegar

1. In a medium bowl or a 4-cup (1 L) storage container, combine cucumbers and green onions.

2. In a cup, stir together sugar, salt and vinegar until sugar is almost dissolved. Pour over cucumbers and stir to mix. Let marinate for at least 20 minutes before serving, or cover and refrigerate for up to 4 days.

tip

Cucumbers will soften and exude more juice the longer this sits. If you like your cukes crisp, eat this salad the first day.

TOMATO BASIL SALAD

SALADS DON'T HAVE to be based on lettuce. Fresh, juicy tomatoes make an alluringly Mediterranean salad accent for all your fave Italian meals.

MAKES 4 SERVINGS

4 large tomatoes, cut into wedges

½ cup (125 mL) packed fresh basil leaves, sliced

2 tbsp (30 mL) balsamic vinegar

2 tbsp (30 mL) extra virgin olive oil

½ tsp (2 mL) salt

1. In a medium bowl, combine tomatoes and basil.
2. In a cup, whisk together vinegar, oil and salt. Pour over tomatoes and toss to coat. Serve immediately.

tip

Tomatoes vary widely in size. The most important thing is to buy the ripest, most fragrant tomatoes; if they are small, add an extra one.

variation

Use Champagne vinegar or red wine vinegar in place of the balsamic.

to pack for lunch

Divide tomatoes and basil among four 2-cup (500 mL) food storage containers. Prepare the dressing and pack 1 tbsp (15 mL) in each of four small airtight containers. Refrigerate for up to 1 day.

TROPICAL FRUIT SALAD
WITH MINT

THIS FRUIT SALAD makes a sweet-tart side dish for meals with their origins in hot climes, like Jamaican or Thai entrées. You'll love the refreshing combo of mango and cucumber.

MAKES 4 SERVINGS

2 mangos, chopped

1 cucumber, peeled (if desired) and chopped

½ cup (125 mL) packed fresh mint leaves, sliced

½ tsp (2 mL) salt

1 tbsp (15 mL) freshly squeezed lime juice

Granulated sugar (optional)

1. In a medium bowl, combine mangos and cucumber. Add mint, salt and lime juice, tossing to coat. Taste a piece of mango; if it is very tart, add a sprinkle of sugar and toss again. Serve immediately or cover tightly and store in the refrigerator for up to 4 days.

tip

Mangos are usually quite green and under-ripe when you buy them, so try to get them a few days before you plan to make this salad and let them sit out at room temperature to ripen. Mangos are ripe when they yield slightly to gentle pressure, and will often give off a fragrance from the stem end.

variation

Replace the mango with 4 cups (1 L) chopped papaya or pineapple.

to pack for lunch

Divide salad among four 1-cup (250 mL) food storage containers. Refrigerate for up to 4 days.

BALSAMIC VINAIGRETTE

SHORT ON TIME? This dressing takes only a minute, it's better than bottled, and it goes with everything!

MAKES ABOUT 1½ CUPS (375 ML)

1-pint (500 mL) glass jar

2 cloves garlic, minced

1 tsp (5 mL) salt

1 tsp (5 mL) freshly ground black pepper

1 tsp (5 mL) granulated sugar

1 cup (250 mL) extra virgin olive oil

½ cup (125 mL) balsamic vinegar

2 tbsp (30 mL) Dijon mustard

1. In jar, combine garlic, salt, pepper, sugar, oil, vinegar and mustard. Seal the jar and shake vigorously. Store in the refrigerator for up to 1 week.

BASIL VINAIGRETTE

YOUR HARD-WORKING BLENDER is perfect for making salad dressings because the speedy blades emulsify the oil and vinegar. Starting the dressing with shallots and basil gives it body and flavor that will jazz up any salad.

MAKES ABOUT 1 CUP (250 ML)

Blender

2 small shallots

1 clove garlic

¼ cup (60 mL) packed fresh basil leaves

1 tsp (5 mL) salt

1 tsp (5 mL) granulated sugar

Pinch freshly ground black pepper

2 tbsp (30 mL) red wine vinegar

1 tbsp (15 mL) Dijon mustard

½ cup (125 mL) extra virgin olive oil

1. Secure the lid on the blender and remove the lid plug. Turn the machine on a low speed and drop in shallots and garlic. Scrape down the container, replace the lid and blend until minced.
2. Add basil, salt, sugar, pepper, vinegar and mustard. Process on high speed until smooth. With the motor running, through the feed tube, very slowly pour in oil and blend until incorporated.
3. Transfer dressing to a jar or other airtight container and store in the refrigerator for up to 1 week.

tips

If your shallots and garlic are not as finely minced as you would like after step 1, don't worry — the job will be finished as you add the oil at the end.

Use this recipe as a template for a dressing of your own invention using other fresh herbs, vinegars and oils. A lovely combo might be fresh dill and white wine vinegar.

SESAME-MISO GARLIC DRESSING

THIS DRESSING DOES double duty as a sauce for just about anything, from stir-fries and grain bowls to wraps and noodles. The tahini, made from sesame seeds, adds protein and calcium, so drizzle freely and enjoy!

MAKES ABOUT 2½ CUPS (625 ML)

Blender (see tip)

4 cloves garlic, chopped

2 tbsp (30 mL) sliced gingerroot

2 tbsp (30 mL) packed brown sugar

1 tsp (5 mL) hot pepper flakes

¾ cup (175 mL) water

¾ cup (175 mL) tahini

¼ cup (60 mL) unseasoned rice vinegar

2 tbsp (30 mL) tamari

2 tbsp (30 mL) toasted (dark) sesame oil

¼ cup (60 mL) white miso

1. In blender, combine garlic, ginger, brown sugar, hot pepper flakes, water, tahini, vinegar, tamari, sesame oil and miso; blend until smooth, scraping down the sides of the container as needed.
2. Transfer dressing to a jar or other airtight container and store in the refrigerator for up to 1 week.

tips

In a pinch, you can make this dressing without a blender. Just mince the garlic and ginger and whisk in the remaining ingredients until smooth.

Try this with other kinds of miso. The darker a miso is, the more intense the flavor will be.

Leave out the garlic if you're worried about having garlic breath.

CREAMY CASHEW DRESSING

FORGET DAIRY-BASED DRESSINGS — this creamy nut-based wonder will steal your heart. Raw cashews purée to a smooth, luscious texture, then transform into a crave-worthy condiment with the addition of a chorus of tart and savory ingredients. A sprinkle of turmeric adds a sunny golden hue, for even more contrast on top of colorful veggies.

MAKES ABOUT 1¼ CUPS (300 ML)

Mini chopper or immersion blender

1 cup (250 mL) raw cashews

Cold water

1 clove garlic, coarsely chopped

2 tbsp (30 mL) nutritional yeast

½ tsp (2 mL) salt

½ tsp (2 mL) ground turmeric

½ cup (125 mL) water (approx.)

2 tbsp (30 mL) apple cider vinegar

1 tbsp (15 mL) white miso

1 tsp (5 mL) Dijon mustard

1. Place cashews in a bowl and add enough cold water to cover. Soak at room temperature for at least 3 hours or overnight. Drain well.
2. In the mini chopper or using an immersion blender in a tall cup, purée cashews, garlic, yeast, salt, turmeric, water, vinegar, miso and mustard until very smooth, scraping down the sides of the container as needed. If it is very thick, add water, 1 tbsp (15 mL) at a time, to make a drizzleable dressing.
3. Transfer dressing to a jar or other airtight container and store in the refrigerator for up to 1 week.

tips

Soaking raw cashews makes them soft, creamy and easy to purée. Don't skip the soak or your dressing will be chunky.

If you have a food processor or a high-speed blender, these appliances will also work well for this recipe. If using the blender, add the water first, then the other ingredients.

variation

For an orange tint, add ½ tsp (2 mL) paprika and 1 tbsp (15 mL) tomato paste, and adjust the final texture with a little more water.

CRISPY KALE
WITH LEMON

ROASTING KALE GIVES it a crisp, sweet quality that may just win over kale skeptics. A quick toss in olive oil and lemon zest makes it sparkle.

MAKES 4 SERVINGS | Preheat oven to 350°F (180°C)

2 large rimmed baking sheets

1 lb (500 g) kale leaves, tough stems and center ribs removed

1 tbsp (15 mL) grated lemon zest

½ tsp (2 mL) salt

1 tbsp (15 mL) olive oil

1. In a large bowl, toss kale with lemon zest, salt and oil. Spread kale evenly on baking sheets.
2. Roast in preheated oven for 10 minutes. Stir and roast for 5 minutes or until crisp. Serve immediately.

tip

Kale stems can be added to soups or thinly sliced to add to salads.

variation

After the kale comes out of the oven, sprinkle with ½ tsp (2 mL) smoked paprika, for a smoky warmth.

LEMONY PESTO BEETS

ROASTED BEETS ARE sweet and intense, and tossing them in a lemony, herby pesto lifts them into the stratosphere. One bite of these will make you crave them again and again.

MAKES 4 SERVINGS

4 cups (1 L) cubed roasted beets (see page 46)

¼ cup (60 mL) Basil Pesto (page 66)

1 tsp (5 mL) grated lemon zest

1. In a large bowl, toss beets with pesto and lemon zest. Serve warm or cold.

 tip

The beets can be stored in airtight containers in the refrigerator for up to 4 days.

BROCCOLINI
WITH PEANUTS

CHOPPED PEANUTS AND tamari are all you need to transform your roasted broccolini into an Asian-inspired side dish. The peanuts add crunch and protein, for a filling and nutritious side dish.

MAKES 4 SERVINGS

3 cups (750 mL) roasted broccolini (see page 47)

Tamari

¼ cup (60 mL) chopped unsalted roasted peanuts

1. In a skillet, warm roasted broccolini over medium heat until heated through. Sprinkle with tamari to taste and peanuts. Serve hot.

PIZZA BREAD

YES, THIS SEEMS a little like junk food, but it's not. It's an easy side dish, topped with a veggie-rich homemade sauce and sprinkled with a nutty, "nooch"-infused homemade Parm. So fire up the oven and make a warm, toasty companion for a creamy soup, such as Creamy Kale Soup with Almonds (page 134).

MAKES 4 SERVINGS | Preheat oven to 400°F (200°C)

Rimmed baking sheet

8-inch (20 cm) baguette, cut in half crosswise and split in half horizontally

1 cup (250 mL) Veggie Spaghetti Sauce (page 61)

2 cups (500 mL) packed spinach leaves, chopped

½ cup (125 mL) Cashew Parmesan (page 69)

1. Place baguette slices, cut side up, on baking sheet and spread sauce over top, dividing evenly. Top with spinach and sprinkle with Parmesan, dividing evenly.
2. Bake in preheated oven for 10 minutes or until browned on top and crisp on the bottom. Serve hot.

variations

For a more nutritious meal, use a whole-grain baguette.

For a chunkier topping, substitute 1 cup (250 mL) finely chopped broccoli for the spinach.

DESSERTS AND SNACKS

APPLE RASPBERRY CRISP WITH ALMONDS

THE GO-TO DESSERT for folks in a hurry has to be the crisp. Instead of mixing and rolling out pie crust, you simply toss the fruit in a baking dish and sprinkle it with a crunchy topping. And you end up with a dessert you won't feel bad about eating.

MAKES 8 SERVINGS | Preheat oven to 400°F (200°C)

12- by 8-inch (30 by 20 cm) casserole dish with lid, lightly oiled

2 lbs (1 kg) Granny Smith apples, peeled and sliced (about 7 cups/1.75 L)

1½ cups (375 mL) raspberries

¼ cup (60 mL) granulated sugar

1 tbsp (15 mL) cornstarch

1 tsp (5 mL) freshly squeezed lemon juice

½ tsp (2 mL) vanilla extract

TOPPING

1 cup (250 mL) large-flake (old-fashioned) rolled oats

¾ cup (175 mL) packed brown sugar

½ cup (125 mL) whole wheat pastry flour

2 tsp (10 mL) ground cinnamon

½ tsp (2 mL) salt

¼ cup (60 mL) canola oil

¼ cup (60 mL) unsweetened apple juice

½ cup (125 mL) almonds, coarsely chopped

1. Place apples and raspberries in prepared casserole dish. Sprinkle with sugar, cornstarch, lemon juice and vanilla; toss to mix.
2. **TOPPING:** In a medium bowl, combine oats, brown sugar, flour, cinnamon and salt.
3. In a cup, stir together oil and apple juice. Stir into oat mixture. Stir in almonds. Sprinkle topping over fruit mixture.
4. Cover and bake in preheated oven for 25 minutes or until fruit is starting to bubble. Uncover and bake for 30 minutes or until top is golden brown and juices are bubbling thickly around the edges. Transfer to a wire rack to cool and serve warm or let cool completely.
5. Store, tightly covered, in the refrigerator for up to 1 week.

tips

Granny Smiths are the go-to apple for baking because they are tart and stay firm after cooking, whereas an eating apple might turn mushy. You can also seek out other interesting baking apples that become available seasonally, like Winesap, Mutsu or Braeburn.

Whole wheat pastry flour has less gluten than standard whole wheat bread flour, so it's ideal for making tender baked goods. Other whole-grain flours with less gluten include white whole wheat, spelt and Kamut; they can be used in place of whole wheat pastry flour with good results.

PEAR CRUMBLE CAKE

CRUMBLE-TOPPED CAKES HAVE real curb appeal: everyone who sees that crunchy topping wants a piece. They are also much easier to make than frosted cakes. The topping on this one is loaded with whole-grain oats and flour, for a nutrition bonus in the form of a delicious treat.

MAKES 16 SERVINGS | Preheat oven to 350°F (180°C)

8-inch (20 cm) square metal baking pan, greased

CRUMBLE

½ cup (125 mL) whole wheat pastry flour

½ cup (125 mL) large-flake (old-fashioned) rolled oats

½ cup (125 mL) packed light brown sugar

1 tsp (5 mL) ground cinnamon

¼ tsp (1 mL) salt

¼ cup (60 mL) melted coconut oil (see tip, page 176)

CAKE

1 cup (250 mL) unsweetened plain almond milk

1 tsp (5 mL) apple cider vinegar

1¼ cups (300 mL) unbleached all-purpose flour

1 tsp (5 mL) baking powder

1 tsp (5 mL) baking soda

¼ tsp (1 mL) salt

½ cup (125 mL) packed brown sugar

¼ cup (60 mL) melted coconut oil

1 tsp (5 mL) vanilla extract

1 cup (250 mL) chopped pears

1. **CRUMBLE:** In a medium bowl, combine flour, oats, brown sugar, cinnamon and salt. Drizzle in coconut oil and mix well. Fluff mixture with your fingers and refrigerate while you prepare the batter.
2. **CAKE:** In a 2-cup (500 mL) measuring cup or bowl, stir together almond milk and vinegar; set aside.
3. In a large bowl, whisk together flour, baking powder, baking soda and salt.
4. Stir brown sugar, coconut oil and vanilla into almond milk mixture, then pour over flour mixture and stir until just moistened. Don't overmix.
5. Scrape batter into prepared pan and arrange pears over top. Sprinkle crumble over pears.
6. Bake in preheated oven for 35 to 40 minutes or until a toothpick inserted in the center comes out with only moist crumbs and no wet batter attached. Transfer cake to a wire rack to cool for 5 minutes, then cut into 16 squares. Store, wrapped or covered tightly, at room temperature for up to 4 days.

variation

Substitute raspberries or chopped apples for the pears.

CHOCOLATE CUPCAKES
WITH FROSTING

CUPCAKES ARE A busy person's friend. This recipe lets you stir up a simple banana-laced batter and bake it in far less time than it would take to make a big cake. Once your chocolate cupcakes are cooled, you can stir up an easy frosting to give them a glossy, decadent finish without a smidge of butter.

MAKES 12 CUPCAKES | Preheat oven to 350°F (180°C)

12-cup muffin pan, lined with paper liners

$3/4$ cup (175 mL) unsweetened plain soy milk

1 tbsp (15 mL) ground flax seeds (flaxseed meal)

$1\frac{1}{4}$ cups (300 mL) unbleached all-purpose flour

1 cup (250 mL) packed light brown sugar

$3/4$ tsp (3 mL) baking soda

$1/2$ tsp (2 mL) salt

$1/4$ cup (60 mL) unsweetened cocoa powder

$1/4$ cup (60 mL) melted coconut oil (see tip, page 176)

$3/4$ cup (175 mL) mashed bananas (about $1\frac{1}{2}$ medium)

1 tsp (5 mL) vanilla extract

FROSTING

$1/2$ cup (125 mL) confectioners' (icing) sugar

$1/2$ cup (125 mL) unsweetened cocoa powder

2 tbsp (30 mL) unsweetened plain soy milk

1 tsp (5 mL) vanilla extract

1. In a cup, stir together milk and flax seeds; set aside.
2. In a large bowl, whisk together flour, brown sugar, baking soda and salt.
3. In a medium bowl, whisk cocoa and coconut oil until blended. Whisk in bananas and vanilla. Whisk in milk mixture until smooth. Gently stir cocoa mixture into flour mixture just until evenly moistened.
4. Divide batter evenly among prepared muffin cups (using rounded $1/4$-cup/60 mL portions).
5. Bake in preheated oven for 20 minutes or until a toothpick inserted in the center of a cupcake comes out with moist crumbs attached. Let cool in pan on a wire rack for 15 minutes, then transfer to the rack to cool completely.
6. **FROSTING:** In a small bowl or a measuring cup, combine sugar and cocoa. Stir in milk and vanilla.
7. Spread a heaping tablespoon (15 mL) of frosting on each cupcake. Store, tightly covered, in the refrigerator for up to 1 week.

tip

You don't need butter for a thick frosting. Stirring in just enough soy milk for a spreadable texture is easy and lower in fat.

variation

MEXICAN CHOCOLATE CUPCAKES: Add 1 tsp (5 mL) ground cinnamon with the salt.

WALNUT BROWNIES
WITH GANACHE

GOING VEGAN DOESN'T mean giving up brownies that melt in your mouth. Your friends will devour these and never notice they're vegan. The fast and easy ganache adds a finishing touch that's as pretty as it is delicious.

MAKES 9 BROWNIES | **Preheat oven to 350°F (180°C)**

8-inch (20 cm) square metal baking pan, greased and lined with parchment paper, leaving a 2-inch (5 cm) overhang on two sides

1½ cups (375 mL) unbleached all-purpose flour

¾ cup (175 mL) unsweetened cocoa powder

¾ cup (175 mL) granulated sugar

2 tbsp (30 mL) arrowroot starch

1 tsp (5 mL) baking powder

¾ tsp (3 mL) salt

1 oz (30 g) unsweetened chocolate, melted (see tip, page 184)

¾ cup (175 mL) pure maple syrup

¾ cup (175 mL) coconut milk

¼ cup (60 mL) melted coconut oil (see tip, page 176)

¼ cup (60 mL) canola oil

1 tbsp (15 mL) vanilla extract

½ cup (125 mL) walnut halves, chopped

GANACHE

¼ cup (60 mL) coconut milk

3 oz (90 g) vegan semisweet chocolate, chopped

1. In a large bowl, whisk together flour, cocoa, sugar, arrowroot, baking powder and salt until no lumps remain.

2. In a medium bowl, whisk together chocolate, maple syrup, coconut milk, coconut oil, canola oil and vanilla. Stir into flour mixture just until evenly moistened. Fold in walnuts.

3. Spread batter in prepared pan.

4. Bake in preheated oven for about 30 minutes or until the top looks cracked and dry and a toothpick inserted in the center comes out with moist crumbs clinging to it. Let cool completely in pan on a wire rack.

5. **GANACHE:** In a small saucepan, warm coconut milk over low heat. Stir in chocolate and heat, stirring, until melted and smooth.

6. Drizzle ganache over cooled cake and refrigerate for about 1 hour or until ganache is firm. Use the parchment overhang to lift out the cake, then cut into 9 squares. Store, tightly covered, in the refrigerator for up to 1 week.

tips

Don't use cold ingredients in step 2; if you do, the chocolate will harden instead of mixing in smoothly.

Semisweet chocolate contains at least 35% cacao. If you go with a cacao percentage higher than 60% in these brownies, they may not be as sweet as you would like.

MATCHA-GLAZED PISTACHIO BLONDIES

MATCHA, MADE FROM steamed and powdered green tea leaves, has a distinctive sweet, slightly bitter flavor that has made matcha lattes a staple of coffee shops. It gives these bars an exotic taste and color, and tints the glaze a lovely shade of green.

MAKES 16 SQUARES | Preheat oven to 350°F (180°C)

8-inch (20 cm) square metal baking pan, greased and lined with parchment paper, leaving a 2-inch (5 cm) overhang on two sides

¾ cup (175 mL) coconut milk

3 tbsp (45 mL) ground flax seeds (flaxseed meal)

1 cup (250 mL) unbleached all-purpose flour

½ cup (125 mL) whole wheat pastry flour

½ tsp (2 mL) baking powder

½ tsp (2 mL) baking soda

½ tsp (2 mL) salt

1 cup (250 mL) packed light brown sugar

½ cup (125 mL) almond butter

½ cup (125 mL) melted coconut oil (see tip, page 176)

1 tsp (5 mL) vanilla extract

½ cup (125 mL) pistachios

½ cup (125 mL) vegan semisweet mini chocolate chips

MATCHA GLAZE

½ cup (125 mL) confectioners' (icing) sugar

½ tsp (2 mL) matcha powder

1½ tbsp (22 mL) unsweetened plain almond milk (approx.)

1. In a cup, stir together coconut milk and flax seeds; set aside.
2. In a large bowl, whisk together all-purpose flour, pastry flour, baking powder, baking soda and salt.
3. In a medium bowl, whisk brown sugar, almond butter, coconut oil and vanilla until smooth. Stir in flax mixture. Pour over flour mixture and stir to combine. Fold in pistachios and chocolate chips.
4. Spread batter in prepared pan.
5. Bake in preheated oven for about 30 minutes or until the top is golden and crinkled and a toothpick inserted in the center comes out with moist crumbs clinging to it. Let cool completely in pan on a wire rack.
6. **GLAZE:** In a measuring cup with a spout, whisk together sugar and matcha powder, then whisk in milk to make a thick, pourable glaze.
7. Drizzle glaze over cooled cake and let set for 30 minutes. Use the parchment overhang to lift out the cake, then cut into 16 squares. Store, tightly covered, at room temperature for up to 4 days.

variation

For more matcha flavor, add 1 tsp (5 mL) matcha powder to the flour mixture.

CARROT SQUARES
WITH LEMON GLAZE

SHREDDED CARROTS MAKE these squares as sweet as candy, and you'll feel virtuous as you indulge in a truly tasty treat.

MAKES 16 SQUARES | Preheat oven to 375°F (190°C)

8-inch (20 cm) square baking pan, lightly oiled

½ cup (125 mL) unsweetened plain soy milk

1 tbsp (15 mL) ground flax seeds (flaxseed meal) or chia seeds

1 tsp (5 mL) freshly squeezed lemon juice

¼ cup (60 mL) melted coconut oil (see tip, page 176)

½ tsp (2 mL) vanilla extract

1¼ cups (300 mL) whole wheat pastry flour

¾ cup (175 mL) packed light brown sugar

1 tsp (5 mL) ground cinnamon

1 tsp (5 mL) ground ginger

½ tsp (2 mL) baking soda

½ tsp (2 mL) salt

1 cup (250 mL) grated carrots

½ cup (125 mL) raisins

LEMON GLAZE

½ cup (125 mL) confectioners' (icing) sugar

1 tbsp (15 mL) freshly squeezed lemon juice (approx.)

1. In a cup, whisk together milk, flax seeds and lemon juice; let stand for 10 minutes. Stir in coconut oil and vanilla.

2. In a large bowl, whisk together flour, brown sugar, cinnamon, ginger, baking soda and salt. Stir in milk mixture until well blended. Stir in carrots and raisins until just combined.

3. Spread batter in prepared pan.

4. Bake in preheated oven for about 25 minutes or until puffed and firm to the touch. Let cool completely in pan on a wire rack.

5. **GLAZE:** Place sugar in a cup and, using a fork, stir in lemon juice to make a thick paste. Add a few more drops of lemon juice until glaze is just pourable.

6. Drizzle glaze over cooled cake. Let stand at room temperature for at least 30 minutes or until set, then cut into 16 squares. Store in an airtight container, or in sandwich bags for packing in lunches, in the refrigerator for up to 1 week.

tip

Whenever you grate carrots, prepare extra to put on salads, in sandwiches or on a bowl meal.

variation

Substitute dried cranberries for the raisins or go nuts with chopped walnuts.

NO-BAKE CHERRY WALNUT CRISPY BARS

THESE ARE A grown-up version of the Rice Krispies bars of your youth. Instead of non-vegan gelatin marshmallows laden with corn syrup, these gems are held together with nut butter and agave nectar and studded with granola, oats, cherries and nuts. No-bake means the kitchen stays cool!

MAKES 12 BARS

13- by 9-inch (33 by 23 cm) baking pan, greased

2 cups (500 mL) prepared granola

2 cups (500 mL) crispy brown rice cereal

1 cup (250 mL) large-flake (old-fashioned) rolled oats

1 cup (250 mL) dried cherries

½ cup (125 mL) walnut halves, coarsely chopped

½ cup (125 mL) packed light brown sugar

⅓ cup (75 mL) agave nectar

¼ cup (60 mL) melted coconut oil (see tip), plus a dab for oiling your hands

½ cup (125 mL) almond butter

1 tsp (5 mL) almond extract

½ tsp (2 mL) salt

1. In a large bowl, combine granola, rice, oats, cherries and walnuts.
2. In a small pot, combine brown sugar, agave nectar and coconut oil. Bring to a boil over medium-high heat, stirring to dissolve sugar, then boil for 1 minute.
3. Remove from heat and whisk in almond butter, almond extract and salt. Pour over granola mixture, using a heavy spoon to mix until evenly coated.
4. Scrape granola mixture into prepared pan. Lightly oil your hands and press mixture into the pan until flat and compressed. Let cool completely, then refrigerate for 1 hour. Cut into 12 bars. Store, tightly covered, at room temperature for up to 1 week.

tip

Coconut oil becomes solid when held at below 70°F (30°C) and is more difficult to measure. To melt it, place the jar in a bowl and pour warm water into the bowl to come up the sides but not to the top of the jar. You can also take the lid off and microwave the jar on High for 1 minute. This does not affect the quality of the oil and can be done whenever you need liquid coconut oil.

CHOCOLATE CHIP OAT COOKIES

THERE'S A REASON chocolate chip cookies are the hands-down favorite cookie. The combination of rich, vanilla-kissed cookie and melting chocolate chips just does it for us. This vegan version is just as good, with puréed dates adding natural sweetness to the dough and a sprinkling of oats for terrific texture.

MAKES 12 LARGE COOKIES | Preheat oven to 350°F (180°C)

Blender

2 baking sheets, lined with parchment paper

1 cup (250 mL) whole wheat pastry flour

1 cup (250 mL) unbleached all-purpose flour

½ cup (125 mL) large-flake (old-fashioned) rolled oats

1 tsp (5 mL) baking soda

½ tsp (2 mL) baking powder

½ tsp (2 mL) salt

½ cup (125 mL) unsweetened apple juice

¼ cup (60 mL) melted coconut oil (see tip, page 176)

1 tbsp (15 mL) vanilla extract

1 cup (250 mL) granulated sugar

½ cup (125 mL) packed pitted dates

1 tbsp (15 mL) flax seeds

1 cup (250 mL) vegan semisweet chocolate chips

1. In a large bowl, whisk together pastry flour, all-purpose flour, oats, baking soda, baking powder and salt.

2. In blender, combine apple juice, coconut oil, vanilla, sugar, dates and flax seeds; purée until smooth, scraping down the sides of the container as needed.

3. Pour apple juice mixture over flour mixture and stir to combine. Fold in chocolate chips.

4. Scoop up scant ¼-cup (60 mL) portions of dough and place 2 inches (5 cm) apart on prepared baking sheets.

5. Bake in preheated oven for 20 minutes, swapping the position of the pans halfway through, until cookies are golden around the edges but still moist-looking in the center. Let cool on pans on wire racks for 5 minutes, then transfer cookies to the racks to cool completely. Store in an airtight container at room temperature for up to 1 week.

tip

Using date purée in the cookies replaces some of the sugar and fat, for a slightly less decadent cookie.

variation

For nutty cookies, add ½ cup (125 mL) chopped walnuts with the chocolate chips.

TRIPLE CHOCOLATE COOKIES

OH YES, THERE'S a lot of chocolate here, answering that craving just as satisfyingly as a buttery cookie would. Cocoa, unsweetened chocolate and brown sugar in the dough give the cookies maximum chocolate flavor, and the melty bits of chopped semisweet chocolate take them over the top.

MAKES 20 COOKIES | Preheat oven to 350°F (180°C)

Large baking sheet, lined with parchment paper

1 cup (250 mL) unbleached all-purpose flour

¼ cup (60 mL) unsweetened cocoa powder

½ tsp (2 mL) baking soda

¼ tsp (1 mL) salt

1 oz (30 g) unsweetened chocolate, coarsely chopped

½ cup (125 mL) melted coconut oil (see tip, page 176)

¾ cup (175 mL) packed light brown sugar

2 tbsp (30 mL) unsweetened plain soy milk

1 tbsp (15 mL) ground flax seeds (flaxseed meal)

2 tsp (10 mL) vanilla extract

3 oz (90 g) vegan semisweet chocolate, coarsely chopped

1. In a large bowl, whisk together flour, cocoa, baking soda and salt.
2. In a small pan over medium heat, melt unsweetened chocolate and coconut oil, stirring until smooth (or melt in a bowl in the microwave). Stir in brown sugar until dissolved. Let cool completely.
3. In a cup, stir together milk and flax seeds; let stand for 5 minutes. Stir into chocolate mixture. Add vanilla, stirring well.
4. Scrape chocolate mixture into flour mixture and stir until well combined. Stir in semisweet chocolate.
5. Scoop up slightly rounded 1-tbsp (15 mL) portions of dough and roll into balls. Place balls 2 inches (5 cm) apart on prepared baking sheet. Using wet palms, flatten dough slightly to ½ inch (1 cm) thick.
6. Bake in preheated oven for 10 minutes or until puffed and dry-looking on top but still soft in the middle. Let cool on pan on a wire rack for 5 minutes, then transfer cookies to the racks to cool completely. Store in an airtight container at room temperature for up to 1 week.

tip

These cookies are best when soft in the middle; don't overbake them or you'll lose that melty quality.

variation

Substitute ½ cup (125 mL) vegan semisweet chocolate chips for the chopped semisweet chocolate.

PEANUT BUTTER RAISIN COOKIES

PEANUT BUTTER AND raisins go together like peanut butter and jelly, so why not put the combo in a cookie and relive your childhood favorite lunchtime treat?

MAKES 14 COOKIES | Preheat oven to 350°F (180°C)

2 baking sheets, lined with parchment paper

½ cup (125 mL) whole wheat pastry flour

½ cup (125 mL) unbleached all-purpose flour

1 tbsp (15 mL) ground flax seeds (flaxseed meal)

½ tsp (2 mL) baking soda

¼ tsp (1 mL) salt

½ cup (125 mL) crunchy natural peanut butter

6 tbsp (90 mL) pure maple syrup

¼ cup (60 mL) canola oil

¾ tsp (3 mL) vanilla extract

¼ cup (60 mL) raisins

1. In a large bowl, whisk together pastry flour, all-purpose flour, flax seeds, baking soda and salt.
2. In a medium bowl, whisk together peanut butter, maple syrup, oil and vanilla. Pour over flour mixture and stir until well combined. Stir in raisins.
3. Scoop up 2-tbsp (30 mL) portions of dough and roll into balls. Place balls 3 inches (7.5 cm) apart on prepared baking sheets. Using wet palms, flatten dough to ¾ inch (2 cm) thick. If desired, press a fork on top of each to make classic crosshatch marks.
4. Bake in preheated oven for 16 minutes, swapping the position of the pans halfway through, until the edges are golden and the cookies are puffed. Let cool on pans on wire racks for 5 minutes, then transfer cookies to the racks to cool completely. Store in an airtight container at room temperature for up to 1 week.

tip

When you bring home a jar of natural peanut butter, store it upside down so that, when you open it, the oil is on the bottom, making it slightly easier to mix.

variation

Try these with almond butter instead of peanut butter, and chunks of almonds instead of raisins.

PEANUT BUTTER THUMBPRINTS
FILLED WITH GANACHE

EACH OF THESE melt-in-your-mouth peanut butter cookies cradles a pool of luscious chocolate cream. Before you get going, make sure you have room in the refrigerator to chill these on the baking sheet.

MAKES 30 COOKIES

2 baking sheets, lined with parchment paper

1 cup (250 mL) unbleached all-purpose flour

¾ cup (175 mL) whole wheat pastry flour

1 tsp (5 mL) baking powder

¼ tsp (1 mL) salt

¾ cup (175 mL) melted coconut oil (see tip, page 176)

½ cup (125 mL) creamy natural peanut butter

½ cup (125 mL) pure maple syrup

1 tsp (5 mL) vanilla extract

GANACHE

2 oz (60 g) vegan semisweet chocolate, coarsely chopped

2 tbsp (30 mL) coconut milk

1. In a large bowl, whisk together all-purpose flour, pastry flour, baking powder and salt.
2. In a medium bowl, whisk together coconut oil, peanut butter, maple syrup and vanilla until well blended. Add to the flour mixture and stir until well combined.
3. Scoop up 1-tbsp (15 mL) portions of dough and roll into balls. Place balls 3 inches (7.5 cm) apart on prepared baking sheets and, using a wet fingertip, make an indentation in the center of each ball. Refrigerate for 30 minutes.
4. Meanwhile, preheat oven to 350°F (180°C).
5. Bake for 14 minutes, swapping the position of the pans halfway through, until golden around the edges. Using the handle of a wooden spoon, press down indentations if they have puffed up. Let cool on pans on wire racks for 5 minutes, then transfer cookies to the racks to cool completely.
6. **GANACHE:** In a small metal bowl set over simmering water, combine chocolate and coconut milk; heat, stirring occasionally, until chocolate is soft, then stir until melted and smooth. Let cool for 5 minutes.
7. Using a small spoon, scoop melted chocolate mixture into the indentation in each cookie. Let cool until chocolate is set. Store in an airtight container in the refrigerator for up to 1 week.

variation

PEANUT BUTTER AND JELLY THUMBPRINTS: Fill the cookies with your favorite jam in place of the ganache. You'll need about ¾ cup (175 mL).

MATCHA AVOCADO SNICKERDOODLES

MATCHA AND AVOCADO conspire to give these tender cookies a hint of green and a distinctive flavor. Eat one as a pick-me-up — you'll get a little boost from the caffeine and sugar without resorting to a full-on double espresso.

MAKES 18 COOKIES | Preheat oven to 375°F (190°C)

2 baking sheets, lined with parchment paper

1/2 cup (125 mL) white whole wheat flour or whole wheat pastry flour

1/2 tsp (2 mL) baking soda

1/2 tsp (2 mL) salt

2 tsp (10 mL) matcha powder, divided

2/3 cup (150 mL) granulated sugar

1/3 cup (75 mL) mashed avocado

1/4 cup (60 mL) melted coconut oil (see tip, page 176)

2 tbsp (30 mL) grated gingerroot

1 tsp (5 mL) vanilla extract

1/2 cup (125 mL) granulated sugar

1. In a large bowl, whisk together flour, baking soda, salt and 1 tsp (5 mL) matcha.
2. In a medium bowl, combine 2/3 cup (150 mL) sugar, avocado, coconut oil, ginger and vanilla, beating with a spoon until very smooth and creamy. Stir into flour mixture until well combined.
3. In a small bowl, combine 1/2 cup (125 mL) sugar and the remaining matcha.
4. Scoop up 1-tbsp (15 mL) portions of dough and roll into balls. Roll each ball in sugar mixture and place balls 2 inches (5 cm) apart on prepared baking sheets.
5. Bake in preheated oven for 12 minutes, swapping the position of the pans halfway through, until cookies are light golden and puffed. Let cool completely on pans on wire racks. Store in an airtight container at room temperature for up to 4 days.

tips

Matcha is made from the first flush of green tea leaves, which are steamed, dried and ground to a fine powder.

Avocado is remarkably rich and sweet, and makes these cookies extra-delicious.

variation

For a more traditional snickerdoodle, substitute ground cinnamon for the matcha powder.

APRICOT SCONES

WHETHER YOU SERVE them with tea or coffee, a plate of scones is a welcoming delight. These easy scones are a perfectly portable breakfast or snack, tastily enhanced by pantry-friendly dried apricots.

MAKES 8 SCONES | Preheat oven to 400°F (200°C)

Bench knife (dough scraper) or chef's knife

Baking sheet, lined with parchment paper

1 ripe banana, mashed

¼ cup (60 mL) unsweetened plain soy milk

1 tsp (5 mL) freshly squeezed lemon juice

1½ cups (375 mL) whole wheat pastry flour

½ cup (125 mL) packed light brown sugar

¼ cup (60 mL) coarse cornmeal

1 tbsp (15 mL) grated lemon zest

2 tsp (10 mL) baking powder

½ tsp (2 mL) salt

½ cup (125 mL) solid coconut oil (see tip, page 183)

½ cup (125 mL) packed dried apricots, chopped

1. In a medium bowl, combine banana, milk and lemon juice. Let stand for 5 minutes to curdle.

2. In a large bowl, combine flour, brown sugar, cornmeal, lemon zest, baking powder and salt, stirring well. Using the coarse holes of a box grater, grate in coconut oil; toss to coat.

3. Pour milk mixture over flour mixture and gently stir to combine. Do not overmix. When the dough is almost formed, fold in apricots.

4. Scrape dough out onto a lightly floured work surface. Form into a disk and flatten to about 1 inch (2.5 cm) thick. Using the bench knife, cut into 8 wedges. Place wedges 2 inches (5 cm) apart on prepared baking sheet.

5. Bake in preheated oven for 15 to 20 minutes or until scones are light golden and firm to the touch. Slide parchment and scones off the pan onto a wire rack and let cool completely. Store, tightly wrapped, in the refrigerator for up to 4 days.

tip

Whole wheat pastry flour is lower in gluten than standard whole wheat flour and makes more tender scones.

variation

Try other dried fruit, such as raisins or cherries, in place of the apricots.

SWEET POTATO PECAN SCONES

TAKE YOUR SWEET potatoes on the road with these pecan-studded scones. The warming spices and hint of maple syrup whisper "Fall," but you can enjoy these any time of year.

MAKES 8 SCONES | Preheat oven to 400°F (200°C)

Bench knife (dough scraper) or chef's knife

Baking sheet, lined with parchment paper

1 cup (250 mL) whole wheat pastry flour

¾ cup (175 mL) unbleached all-purpose flour

1 tbsp (15 mL) baking powder

1 tbsp (15 mL) ground cinnamon

½ tsp (2 mL) salt

¼ cup (60 mL) solid coconut oil (see tip)

1 cup (250 mL) mashed baked sweet potato (see page 45)

¼ cup (60 mL) pure maple syrup

¼ cup (60 mL) unsweetened plain soy milk

½ cup (125 mL) chopped pecans

1. In a large bowl, whisk together pastry flour, all-purpose flour, baking powder, cinnamon and salt. Using the coarse holes of a box grater, grate in coconut oil; toss to coat.
2. In a medium bowl, whisk together sweet potato, maple syrup and milk. Stir into flour mixture until just combined. Fold in pecans.
3. Scrape dough out onto a lightly floured work surface. Form into a disk and flatten to about 1 inch (2.5 cm) thick. Using the bench knife, cut into 8 wedges. Place wedges 2 inches (5 cm) apart on prepared baking sheet.
4. Bake in preheated oven for 20 to 25 minutes or until scones are golden around the edges and firm to the touch. Slide parchment and scones off the pan onto a wire rack and let cool completely. Store in an airtight container in the refrigerator for up to 1 week.

tip

To measure solid coconut oil, melt it (see tip, page 176), measure out the amount you need, then place the measuring cup in the freezer to solidify the oil again.

CHOCOLATE AVOCADO PUDDING

IF YOU THINK avocados are only for guacamole and savory foods, think again. The tropical countries where avocados flourish all have a tradition of using avocados in sweets, and why not? They are rich and sweet to begin with, and easily make the switch from dip to pudding with a little chocolate and maple to help them along.

MAKES 4 SERVINGS

Blender or food processor

4 large ripe avocados (about 1½ lbs/750 g)

¼ cup (60 mL) unsweetened cocoa powder

¼ tsp (1 mL) salt

6 tbsp (90 mL) pure maple syrup

¼ cup (60 mL) unsweetened plain almond milk

2 tsp (10 mL) vanilla extract

3 oz (90 g) bittersweet (dark) chocolate, melted (see tip) and cooled

2 cups (500 mL) raspberries

1. In blender, purée avocados until smooth, scraping down the sides of the container as needed. Add cocoa, salt, maple syrup, almond milk and vanilla; purée until smooth. Scrape in chocolate and purée to combine.
2. Transfer to an airtight container and refrigerate for at least 1 hour or until cold. Serve topped with raspberries.

tips

To melt chocolate, place coarsely chopped chocolate in a microwave-safe bowl and microwave on High for 1 minute. Stir, then microwave on High in 30-second intervals, stirring between each, until melted and smooth.

This can be a showy dessert, composed in a wine glass or small bowl, surrounded by raspberries, or you can pack it in a small container for a dose of comfort at work.

This pudding can double as a decadent-seeming dip for strawberries or orange segments.

The cooled pudding can be stored, tightly covered, in the refrigerator for up to 4 days.

CHAI SPICE RICE PUDDING

THIS RECIPE IS pure comfort food, with soft rice grains plumped in a sweet, spiced, milky pudding. Brown rice cooks to a soft, sticky finish and never falls apart as white rice does, giving this pudding a hint of chewiness as well as delightful creaminess.

MAKES 4 SERVINGS | **Preheat oven to 375°F (190°C)**

12- by 8-inch (30 by 20 cm) casserole dish, lightly oiled

3 cups (750 mL) cooked medium-grain brown rice (see page 53)

½ cup (125 mL) raisins

1 tsp (5 mL) grated lemon zest

1 tsp (5 mL) ground cinnamon

½ tsp (2 mL) ground cloves

¼ tsp (1 mL) ground cardamom

¼ tsp (1 mL) ground nutmeg

1 cup (250 mL) unsweetened plain soy milk

¼ cup (60 mL) pure maple syrup

½ tsp (2 mL) vanilla extract

1. In a large bowl, combine rice, raisins, lemon zest, cinnamon, cloves, cardamom, nutmeg, milk, maple syrup and vanilla. Spoon into prepared casserole dish.
2. Bake in preheated oven for 25 to 30 minutes or until top is slightly browned and liquids are bubbling around the edges. Let cool slightly and serve warm.

tips

If you don't have cooked brown rice on hand, simply cook 1 cup (250 mL) rice in 2 cups (500 mL) water, with a pinch of salt.

The cooled pudding can be stored, tightly covered, in the refrigerator for up to 4 days.

variation

Substitute cooked black rice (see page 52) or barley (see page 49) for the brown rice.

APPENDIX: STORING FOODS

It's important to keep food safe by cooling and storing it properly. Don't rush hot foods to the refrigerator. Let your beans, grains, roasted veggies and baked goods cool to room temperature before refrigerating them. The reason for this is two-fold. First, hot food radiates heat and steam inside the refrigerator, putting all your food at risk and creating a moist environment for mold to grow. Second, many foods need to release heat and moisture to stop cooking, and putting a lid on them will make them soggy or overcooked. I like to transfer hot food to its final container and let it stand on a wire rack until it cools to room temperature.

Label containers with the recipe title, or a description of their contents, and the date. You may think you'll remember, but it's better to know for sure. You don't want to take a container to work for lunch, only to find that it's your bean prep for the week. I find it works best to label containers while the food is still warm; if you wait until a glass or metal container is in the refrigerator and cold, the tape will often slide right off.

Storage times are provided with many of the recipes. It's up to you whether you want to push it a day, but don't risk food-borne illness. If you think you won't get to something, freeze it; as long as it doesn't contain raw vegetables or lettuce, it will probably still be good when you thaw it out.

MANAGING INVENTORY

Always follow proper rotational procedure and use the oldest foods first. Since you are prepping one week at a time, prepped food should all be eaten, or frozen, before you cook for the next week. When you buy new pantry items, pull older cans and bottles to the front and put the new ones at the rear. That way, it's first in, first out.

INDEX

Library and Archives Canada Cataloguing in Publication

Title: Vegan meal prep : a 5-week plan with 125 ready-to-go recipes / Robin Asbell.
Names: Asbell, Robin, author.
Description: Includes index.
Identifiers: Canadiana 20190047461 | ISBN 9780778806301 (softcover)
Subjects: LCSH: Vegan cooking. | LCGFT: Cookbooks.
Classification: LCC TX837 .A83 2019 | DDC 641.5/6362—dc23